s*upesoup*

Caroline Dumas

soupesoup

65 soups
40 salads
40 sandwiches
and desserts . . .

**photos by
Dominique Lafond**

HarperCollins*PublishersLtd*

For Alexia and Clara

—

I grew up in Beauce, a quiet yet friendly village in Quebec where large families are common and where people take the time to be together and to share with each other. I had a beautiful childhood, with many happy memories of family meals drenched in maple syrup! At the age of seven, I read the cookbook *Fermières de Saint-Côme*, written by some of the women of Beauce. For me, it was more than just a book— it was a novel. In fact, I vividly remember its blue cover. In reading the book, I just wanted to understand and learn what the authors cooked for their families. And so, very early in life, I too began experimenting with food and creating recipes. Today, in the same spirit of sharing and creativity as the women of my village, I am proud to share this cookbook with you.

I tend to cook with spontaneity, moving around the kitchen quickly, often surprising myself with the result. I acquired this sense of urgency in the kitchen by working as a canteen cook on movie sets. Quickly yet effectively, I prepared and cooked "little miracles" on the spot, and received many compliments from the movie crews who were enjoying the pleasures and benefits of a delicious and healthy cuisine. Then came the idea of a restaurant for soups: a place that was to be warm and comforting, a place where you would find soups, stews and dishes just like my mother's . . . It seemed to me that there was, indeed, a place for Soupesoup in this country full of snow!

I worked, cooked, created . . . and shopped! I stirred soups and lifted countless pots of chicken carcasses and beef bones and crates and crates of vegetables! I shopped endlessly to find the best-quality bread and meats for my sandwiches, I met several suppliers of vegetables, and I sourced the finest chocolate and maple syrup for my desserts. It was important to me that I have only the freshest and most natural products.

Over time, I realized I could do things more efficiently. I developed a different way to start my soups: first caramelizing the onion, leek and garlic, then adding stronger-tasting fresh herbs like thyme and rosemary, and then finally incorporating vegetables one by one with just a little water. Using this gradual method, and ending with a handful of fresh herbs, I no longer have to prepare meat broth. I save time, and my soups triumph in flavour and nutritional properties.

While my first daughter learned to read in the kitchen, my second was almost born in a pot! The day I went into labour, Reema, my colleague, posted a sign on the restaurant door: "Closed. Left to give birth!" After only one week off, I was back in the kitchen. Luckily, my eldest daughter helped out tremendously. The result? A baby perfumed in caramelized onions and roasted peppers! What a wonderful time in my life, with so much laughter and so much happiness.

I love what I do—cook, chat with my colleagues, and discover food artisans, local farmers, and cheesemongers, all of whom produce organic foods simply because they believe in it. My greatest reward is all of my loyal customers, but my greatest pleasure would be to find that some of my recipes have become part of your own repertoire!

×

① Soups

Samedi · Dim

Cuire le bœuf ·
· poeler les
champignons · fair
· couper les
tomates séchées
· tailler le mengrai
· tailler le provolon
· s'assurer d'avoir
des oignons
caramélis
· couper le

Mango Lassi

—

3 large ripe mangoes, coarsely chopped

½ cup (125 mL) yogurt

⅓ cup (80 mL) 35% cream (optional)

Juice of 1½ limes

1 teaspoon (5 mL) finely chopped bird's eye chili or red pepper flakes

1 to 2 cups (250 to 500 mL) water

Sea salt and freshly cracked pepper

Fresh herb sprigs or thin strips of sweet red pepper

—

Variations

For a change of flavours, add 1 tsp (5 mL) nigella seeds (see p. 20) or 1 tsp (5 mL) grated fresh ginger simmered in 1 tbsp (15 mL) olive oil.

—

PURÉE all ingredients, except herbs or red pepper, in a blender, adding water gradually to reach desired consistency. Season.

REFRIGERATE for at least 2 hours. Serve garnished with fresh herbs or red pepper.

×

Cold Mango Soup with Cucumber and Lime

—

2 mangoes, coarsely chopped

3 English cucumbers, peeled and coarsely chopped

Juice of 2 limes

2 small garlic cloves

1 chili pepper, seeded

1 to 2 cups (250 to 500 mL) yogurt

1 cup (250 mL) water

½ cup (125 mL) basil leaves

Sea salt and freshly cracked pepper

Basil leaves for garnish

Ice cubes

—

Variation

You can make a similar soup by replacing the mangoes with white peaches and the basil with tarragon.

—

PURÉE all the ingredients, except basil garnish and ice, in a blender. Season.

SERVE with a few basil leaves and a couple of ice cubes in each bowl.

Chilled Fig Soup with Feta and Mint

—

10 fresh figs

2½ cups (625 mL) water

¼ cup (60 mL) yogurt

3 tablespoons (45 mL) white balsamic vinegar

Juice of 2 limes

8 mint leaves

1 tablespoon (15 mL) chopped chives

Sea salt and freshly cracked pepper

¼ cup (60 mL) crumbled feta cheese (preferably sheep's milk)

Olive oil

4 thyme sprigs

—

Variation

To achieve a different, softer flavour, replace the mint in any fruit soup with an equal amount of lemon balm heated in 1 to 2 tbsp (15 to 30 mL) agave nectar.

—

PURÉE all the ingredients, except feta, oil and thyme, in a blender. Season.

REFRIGERATE for 1 hour. Garnish each serving with feta, drizzle with oil and top with a sprig of thyme and some cracked pepper.

×

Chilled Peach Soup with Basil

—

4 or 5 white or regular peaches, pitted

½ medium chili pepper, very finely chopped

1 cup (250 mL) yogurt

½ cup (125 mL) water

6 or 7 basil leaves

Juice of 2 limes

1 teaspoon (15 mL) nigella seeds (optional)

Sea salt and freshly cracked pepper

6 chives, chopped, or edible flowers

—

Nigella seeds

These small black cumin seeds are lemony in aroma and slightly spicy. They are primarily used to flavour naan bread.

—

PURÉE all the ingredients, except chives, in a blender.

REFRIGERATE for 30 minutes. Season and garnish with chives or flowers just before serving.

×

Refreshing Honeydew and Thyme Soup

22

—

1 tablespoon (15 mL) chopped thyme or mint

4 cups (1 L) honeydew melon, cubed

¼ cup (60 mL) yogurt

Sea salt and freshly cracked pepper

—

PURÉE all ingredients in a blender. Season.

REFRIGERATE until chilled.

×

Spiced Watermelon Soup

—

1 seedless watermelon, cut into pieces

Juice of 3 limes

1 teaspoon (5 mL) garam masala

1 teaspoon (5 mL) turmeric

A pinch of cayenne

Sea salt and freshly cracked pepper

—

PURÉE all ingredients in a blender. Season.

REFRIGERATE until chilled.

×

Cold Cantaloupe Soup with Orange Blossom Water

—

2 tablespoons (30 mL) olive oil

1 tablespoon (15 mL) curry powder

½ sweet red pepper, julienned

¾ cup (180 mL) red onion, finely chopped

1½ cups (375 mL) coarsely chopped sweet potato

4 cups (1 L) boiling water

1 teaspoon (5 mL) orange blossom water

Sea salt and freshly cracked pepper

Red pepper flakes, to taste

1 cup (250 mL) diced cantaloupe

½ cup (125 mL) chopped cilantro

½ cup (125 mL) chopped basil

Toasted sliced almonds

—

HEAT oil in a small pan over medium heat. Add curry powder, red pepper and onion and cook for 5 to 10 minutes, until onion is soft.

ADD sweet potatoes, water and orange blossom water. Season with salt, pepper and red pepper flakes. Simmer for 10 to 15 minutes or until sweet potato is tender.

PURÉE in a blender. Stir in cantaloupe.

REFRIGERATE for 2 hours. Season and garnish with cilantro, basil and almonds just before serving.

×

Fresh Melon Soup with Ginger

—

1 tablespoon (15 mL) olive oil

1 teaspoon (5 mL) fennel seeds

1 inch (2.5 cm) fresh ginger, grated

1 melon (any kind), peeled and cut into chunks

1 cup (250 mL) seedless green grapes

¼ cup (60 mL) yogurt

1 teaspoon (5 mL) chopped mint

Juice of 1 lime

Sea salt and freshly cracked pepper

Whole mint leaves or 1 teaspoon (5 mL) chopped candied ginger

—

HEAT oil in a small skillet over low heat. Add fennel seeds and ginger; cook for 3 minutes.

PURÉE fennel mixture with all ingredients, except whole mint leaves, in a blender, adding a little water if necessary. Season.

REFRIGERATE for 1 hour. Serve garnished with mint leaves or chopped candied ginger.

×

Summer Cucumber Soup with Blueberries and Herbs

—

2 tablespoons (30 mL) olive oil

3 garlic cloves, chopped

2 English cucumbers, partly peeled and coarsely chopped

3 cups (750 mL) water

1 tablespoon (15 mL) grainy mustard (optional)

Juice of ½ lemon

3 tablespoons (45 mL) yogurt

3 tablespoons (45 mL) chopped watercress (optional)

¼ cup (60 mL) chopped tarragon, dill or chives

Sea salt and freshly cracked pepper

½ cup (125 mL) blueberries

—

HEAT oil in a skillet over low heat. Add garlic and cook for 3 minutes or until softened.

PURÉE garlic and remaining ingredients, except blueberries and 1 tsp (5 mL) of the herbs, in a blender. Season.

REFRIGERATE for 1 hour. Add blueberries and garnish with remaining herbs just before serving.

×

Cold Avocado Soup with Tomatoes

—

4 ripe avocados

Juice of 1 to 2 limes

2 small garlic cloves

½ to 1 chili pepper, chopped, or a pinch of cayenne

1 cup (250 mL) yogurt

1 to 2 cups (250 to 500 mL) water

½ cup (125 mL) cilantro leaves

Sea salt and freshly cracked pepper

3 chives or 1 green onion, chopped

3 cherry tomatoes, quartered

—

PURÉE all ingredients, except water, a few leaves of cilantro, chives and tomatoes, in a blender. Add water gradually until desired consistency is achieved. Season.

REFRIGERATE for 1 hour. Garnish each bowl with remaining cilantro, chives and a few tomato wedges just before serving.

×

Chilled Tomato and Fennel Soup

—

2 tablespoons (30 mL) olive oil

5 garlic cloves

1 teaspoon (5 mL) fennel seeds

1 onion, finely chopped

3 tomatoes, diced

1 celery stalk, finely chopped

4 cups (1 L) boiling water

1 cup (250 mL) natural apple juice (optional)

Sea salt and freshly cracked pepper

1 fennel bulb, thinly sliced using a mandoline

—

HEAT oil in a saucepan over medium heat. Add garlic, fennel seeds and onion; cook for 5 minutes. Add tomatoes and simmer for another 2 minutes.

ADD celery, water and apple juice, if desired. Season. Simmer for 10 minutes or until vegetables are tender.

PURÉE in a blender. Stir in fennel.

REFRIGERATE for 2 hours.

×

Tomato Soup with Spicy Cucumber

1 tablespoon (15 mL) olive oil

2 garlic cloves, chopped

2 cups (500 mL) diced tomatoes

1 cucumber, cut into pieces

1 cup (250 mL) basil leaves

½ cup (125 mL) mint leaves

1 cup (250 mL) parsley leaves

½ medium chili pepper

Juice of 1 lemon

Sea salt and freshly cracked pepper

HEAT oil in a saucepan over medium heat. Add garlic and tomatoes; cook for 10 minutes or until tomatoes begin to stew.

BLEND tomato mixture with remaining ingredients in a blender until coarsely processed. Season.

SERVE hot or refrigerate for 2 hours to serve cold.

×

Cream of Tomato and Basil Soup

7 tomatoes, quartered

Sea salt and freshly cracked pepper

3 tablespoons (45 mL) olive oil

1 tablespoon (15 mL) butter

2 onions, finely chopped

4 garlic cloves, chopped

2 to 3 cups (500 to 750 mL) boiling water

15 basil leaves, chopped

⅔ cup (160 mL) 35% cream

PREHEAT oven to 375°F (190°C).

PLACE tomato wedges on a baking sheet. Season and drizzle with 1 tbsp (15 mL) oil. Bake for 25 minutes to sweeten them.

HEAT remaining 2 tbsp (30 mL) oil and butter in a skillet over medium-high heat. Add onions and garlic; sauté for 10 minutes or until caramelized.

DISCARD tomato skins and coarsely chop flesh. Purée tomatoes with onion mixture in a blender, adding water until desired consistency is achieved.

STIR in basil and cream. Serve hot.

×

Beet Soup with Tomato and Orange

—

2 tablespoons (30 mL) olive oil

½ red onion, minced

2 tablespoons (30 mL) grated fresh ginger

4 cups (1 L) boiling water

1 cup (250 mL) crushed tomatoes (fresh or canned)

1 cup (250 mL) diced peeled, beets

Zest and juice of 2 oranges (or 1 tablespoon/ 15 mL frozen orange juice concentrate)

¼ cup (60 mL) chopped basil

Sea salt and freshly cracked pepper

—

HEAT oil in a medium saucepan over medium heat. Add onion and ginger; cook for 10 minutes or until caramelized.

STIR in remaining ingredients except basil. Cover and cook for 15 to 20 minutes or until beets are tender. Add basil and season.

SERVE hot or refrigerate for at least 2 hours to serve cold.

×

Papaya Soup with Ginger

—

1 tablespoon (15 mL) butter

¾ cup (180 mL) finely chopped red onion

2 teaspoons (10 mL) grated fresh ginger

½ teaspoon (2 mL) finely chopped bird's eye chili

1 teaspoon (5 mL) ground allspice

4 cups (1 L) cubed papaya

2 cups (500 mL) boiling water

⅔ cup (160 mL) milk

6 tablespoons (90 mL) 35% cream (optional)

3 chives, chopped

—

MELT butter in a large saucepan over medium-high heat. Add onion, ginger, chili and allspice; sauté for 5 minutes.

ADD papaya, water and milk. Bring to a boil, then immediately remove from heat.

PURÉE in a blender. Add cream, if desired.

SERVE hot or refrigerate for at least 2 hours to serve cold. Garnish with chives.

×

Tomato Soup with Ginger

—

3 lb (1.5 kg) tomatoes, quartered

1 tablespoon (15 mL) cane sugar (optional)

Sea salt and freshly cracked pepper

4 tablespoons (60 mL) olive oil

1 small red onion, chopped

1 inch (2.5 cm) fresh ginger, grated

1 garlic clove, minced

1 teaspoon (5 mL) ground cumin

—

PREHEAT oven to 375°F (190°C).

PLACE tomato wedges on a baking sheet. Sprinkle with sugar, if desired, and salt and pepper. Drizzle with 2 tbsp (30 mL) oil. Bake for 25 minutes to sweeten them.

HEAT remaining 2 tbsp (30 mL) oil in a skillet over medium heat. Cook onion, ginger, garlic and cumin until onion is tender, about 5 minutes.

DISCARD tomato skins. Purée tomatoes and onion mixture in a blender. Dilute as needed with a little water. Season.

SERVE hot or refrigerate for 2 hours to serve cold.

×

Lemon Detox Minestrone

—

4 cups (1 L) water

3 thyme sprigs

1 tablespoon (15 mL) cane sugar

Juice of ½ lemon

1 carrot, diced

1 celery stalk, diced

½ leek, white part only, diced

½ fennel bulb, trimmed and diced

Sea salt and freshly cracked pepper

½ cup (125 mL) shaved Parmesan cheese

4 basil leaves

—

Note

Of course, the Parmesan is there for fun, not for detox!

—

BOIL water in a saucepan. Add thyme, sugar, lemon juice and vegetables. Season with salt.

SIMMER over medium heat for 7 minutes or until vegetables are tender. Remove thyme sprigs.

GARNISH with Parmesan and basil and season to taste.

×

Soup with Herbs

—

2 tablespoons (30 mL) olive oil

1 leek, chopped

4 cups (1 L) chicken stock
(see below)

3 cups (750 mL) baby spinach

1 cup (250 mL) watercress

½ cup (125 mL) cilantro leaves

½ cup (125 mL) mint leaves

½ cup (125 mL) basil leaves

Juice of ½ lemon

Sea salt and freshly cracked
pepper

—

Chicken Stock

In a large saucepan, combine
1 medium chicken, 2 coarsely
chopped carrots, 1 leek, washed
and slit lengthwise, 3 celery stalks
cut into 2 or 3 pieces, 1 onion
pierced with 3 cloves, 3 thyme
sprigs (or a bouquet garni) and
15 whole peppercorns. Pour
in enough water to cover the
ingredients, bring to a boil
and simmer for 1½ to 2 hours,
occasionally skimming foam from
the surface. Strain and add salt
to taste, if desired (it's best to
add salt as needed when using
the stock). Reserve the cooked
chicken for sandwich fillings,
salads and soups.

—

HEAT oil in a large saucepan over medium heat. Add leek and 1 tbsp (15 mL) water. Cook for 3 minutes or until softened but not browning.

ADD stock. Bring to a boil, then immediately remove from heat.

STIR in spinach, watercress and herbs. Immediately purée in a blender.

SEASON with lemon juice, salt and pepper.

×

Broccoli Cheddar Soup

—

4 cups (1 L) water

12 cups (3 L) broccoli florets

½ cup (125 mL)
grated sharp Cheddar cheese

Sea salt and freshly
cracked pepper

—

BOIL the water in a large saucepan. Add broccoli and cook, covered, for 5 minutes or until tender. Drain, reserving the cooking water.

PURÉE broccoli in a blender, adding most of the Cheddar (keeping some for garnish) and enough cooking water to reach desired consistency.

SEASON and garnish with remaining Cheddar just before serving.

×

Serves 4

Cauliflower Soup with Padano

—

4 cups (1 L) water

12 cups (3 L)
cauliflower florets

½ cup (125 mL)
grated Grana Padano or
Parmesan cheese

Sea salt and freshly
cracked pepper

—

BOIL the water in a large saucepan. Add cauliflower and cook, covered, for 10 minutes or until tender. Drain, reserving the cooking water.

PURÉE cauliflower in a blender, adding most of the Grana Padano (keeping some for garnish) and enough cooking water to reach desired consistency.

SEASON and garnish with remaining Grana Padano just before serving.

×

Asparagus Soup with Emmental

44

—

2 thick slices bread

1 to 2 garlic cloves, peeled

2 tablespoons (30 mL) olive oil

25 asparagus spears, trimmed

4 cups (1 L) water

½ cup (125 mL) grated Emmental cheese

Sea salt and freshly cracked pepper

—

RUB bread slices with garlic. Cut into small cubes and fry in the oil for 5 minutes or until croutons are golden.

BOIL the water in a large skillet. Add asparagus and a little salt and cook, covered, for 10 minutes or until tender. Drain, reserving the cooking water.

PURÉE asparagus in a blender, adding most of the Emmental (keeping some for garnish) and enough cooking water to reach desired consistency. Season and serve topped with remaining Emmental and garlic croutons.

×

Serves 6

Zucchini Soup with Padano

—

2 tablespoons (30 mL) olive oil

6 zucchini, cut into pieces

1 onion, chopped

2 garlic cloves, chopped

3 to 4 cups (750 mL to 1 L) boiling water

½ cup (125 mL) grated Grana Padano

¼ cup (60 mL) chopped tarragon, basil or mint (optional)

Sea salt and freshly ground pepper

—

HEAT oil in a large saucepan over medium-high heat. Sauté zucchini, onion and garlic for 5 to 10 minutes, until softened.

ADD water, reduce heat to medium and simmer for 10 minutes or until zucchini is tender.

STIR in Grana Padano and herb, if desired. Purée in a blender. Season.

×

Sweet Potato Soup with Lime

—

4 medium sweet potatoes, peeled and diced

4 to 5 cups (1 to 1.25 L) water

Juice of 2 limes

Sea salt and freshly cracked pepper

1 green onion, sliced on the diagonal

¼ cup (60 mL) chopped cilantro

—

Variation

Add just a little water and blend the sweet potatoes into a mash to use as a side dish for fish.

—

BOIL sweet potatoes in the water for 10 minutes or until tender. Drain, reserving the cooking water.

PURÉE potatoes in a blender, gradually adding enough cooking water to reach desired consistency.

STIR in lime juice and season. Serve garnished with green onion and cilantro.

×

Squash Soup with Apples

—

3 tablespoons (45 mL) olive oil

1 medium butternut squash, peeled, seeded and cut into pieces

2 carrots, cut into chunks

1 onion, coarsely chopped

1 leek, coarsely chopped

3 garlic cloves, crushed

3 apples, cored and cut into pieces (cut a few pieces into matchsticks for garnish)

2 potatoes, peeled and cut into pieces

3 thyme sprigs

5 cups (1.25 L) boiling water

Sea salt and freshly cracked pepper

—

HEAT 2 tbsp (30 mL) oil in a large saucepan over medium heat. Cook all ingredients, except the water and apple garnish, for 5 minutes.

ADD boiling water, reduce heat and simmer for 20 minutes or until vegetables are tender. Remove thyme sprigs.

PURÉE in a blender. Season.

GARNISH each bowl with remaining apple and a drizzle of olive oil.

Pumpkin Soup with Cranberry Coulis

—

2 tablespoons (30 mL) olive oil

5 garlic cloves, chopped

1 leek, chopped

3 cups (750 mL) boiling water

1 celery stalk, cut into pieces

3 cups (750 mL) cubed pumpkin

Leaves from 1 thyme sprig

2 to 3 sage leaves

½ teaspoon (2 mL) red pepper flakes

Sea salt and freshly cracked pepper

—

Cranberry Coulis

1 cup (250 mL) water

1 cup (250 mL) frozen cranberries

⅓ cup (80 mL) cane sugar

—

HEAT oil in a large saucepan over medium heat. Cook garlic and leeks without browning for 5 to 10 minutes, moistening with 1 tbsp (15 mL) water if necessary.

ADD remaining ingredients. Simmer, covered, for 20 minutes or until vegetables are tender. Purée in a blender. Season and reserve.

HEAT water for coulis in a medium saucepan. Add cranberries and sugar. Bring to a boil, then simmer, uncovered, for 10 minutes or until cranberries begin to stew. Purée in a blender.

GARNISH soup with cranberry coulis.

×

Julien's Gazpacho

—

1 cucumber

2 celery stalks

2 sweet peppers
(yellow, red or orange)

½ red onion

1 cup (250 mL)
chopped cilantro

2 garlic cloves,
finely chopped

½ chili pepper, finely
chopped (or ½ teaspoon/
2 mL piri-piri sauce)

Juice of 1 lemon and 1 lime

4 cups (1 L) vegetable juice

Fresh Herb Coulis
(optional; p. 276)

Sea salt and freshly
cracked pepper

—

CHOP all vegetables into a small dice.

TOSS vegetables with remaining
ingredients, except herb coulis. Season.

REFRIGERATE at least 2 hours and serve as
is or topped with coulis.

×

Andalusian Gazpacho

—

8 tomatoes, quartered

1 cucumber, unpeeled,
cut into pieces

1 sweet red pepper,
cut into pieces

2 garlic cloves,
coarsely chopped

¼ baguette, cut into pieces

3 tablespoons (45 mL)
sherry vinegar

2 tablespoons (30 mL)
olive oil

Sea salt and freshly
cracked pepper

Croutons for garnish

—

Variation

To add some crunch,
garnish each bowl of
gazpacho with 1 tbsp
(15 mL) mixed finely
chopped red pepper,
cucumber and red onion.

—

TOSS together all ingredients, except olive oil, in a large bowl and refrigerate for at least 24 hours.

PURÉE in a blender, then pass through a fine-mesh sieve. Season.

GARNISH with olive oil and croutons just before serving.

×

Cream of Roasted Red Pepper Soup

—

4 garlic cloves, unpeeled

2 to 3 sweet red peppers, halved

2 tablespoons (30 mL) olive oil

1 onion, finely chopped

1 celery stalk, finely chopped

½ teaspoon (2 mL) smoked paprika

1 cup (250 mL) diced potatoes

4 cups (1 L) boiling water

Sea salt and freshly cracked pepper

¼ cup (60 mL) chopped parsley

Juice of 1 lime

—

Variations

You can replace the potato with 1 cup (250 mL) chopped tomatoes. Add 2 cups (500 mL) boiling water, then add more if needed.

You can also replace the potato with croutons, which saves you having to simmer the soup for longer to cook the potato.

—

PREHEAT oven to 400°F (200°C).

PLACE garlic and peppers on a baking sheet. Brush with 1 tbsp (15 mL) oil. Bake for 15 to 20 minutes or until peppers are charred.

SQUEEZE out garlic flesh from peel. Remove skin from peppers (you don't need them to be perfectly peeled; a little bit of burnt skin is tasty).

HEAT remaining 1 tbsp (15 mL) oil in a saucepan over medium heat. Cook onion and celery with paprika for 5 to 10 minutes or until softened and translucent.

ADD potatoes, roasted peppers, garlic and boiling water. Simmer, covered, for 15 minutes or until potato is tender.

PURÉE in a blender. Season.

GARNISH with parsley. This soup can be served hot or cold with lime juice.

×

Eggplant Soup with Gremolata

—

¼ cup (60 mL) olive oil

1 small onion, chopped

1 garlic clove, chopped

2 medium eggplants, peeled and coarsely chopped

3 cups (750 mL) boiling water

½ cup (125 mL) yogurt or 35% cream

Sea salt and freshly cracked pepper

Gremolata (see below)

—

Gremolata

In a bowl, mix the zest of ½ orange and ½ lemon with 1 cup (250 mL) chopped parsley and 1 clove garlic, minced.

—

HEAT oil in a saucepan over medium-high heat. Sauté onion, garlic and eggplant for 7 minutes or until eggplant has browned.

ADD boiling water. Reduce heat to medium and simmer, covered, for 10 minutes.

REMOVE soup from heat and stir in yogurt. Purée in a blender. Season.

GARNISH each bowl with 1 tbsp (15 mL) gremolata.

×

Spanish Almond Soup

—

1 whole head garlic

¼ cup (60 mL) olive oil

2 onions, chopped

1 tablespoon (15 mL)
ground cumin
+ 1 tablespoon (15 mL)
smoked paprika

2 large potatoes,
peeled and cut into pieces

⅓ cup (80 mL)
ground almonds

1 tablespoon (15 mL)
balsamic vinegar

4 cups (1 L) boiling water

½ cup (125 mL) 35% cream

Sea salt and freshly
cracked pepper

⅓ cup (80 mL)
sliced almonds

—

PREHEAT oven to 400°F (200°C). Drizzle garlic with a little of the oil, wrap in foil and bake for 30 minutes. Extract cloves, mash into a paste and reserve.

HEAT remaining oil in a large saucepan over medium heat. Cook onion, cumin and paprika for 5 minutes or until fragrant.

ADD potatoes, ground almonds, vinegar and water. Simmer for 10 minutes or until potatoes are tender.

STIR in garlic and cream. Simmer for 3 minutes, then purée in a blender. Season.

TOAST sliced almonds in a dry pan until golden. Use to garnish just before serving.

×

Scarlet Minestrone

—

3 tablespoons (45 mL)
olive oil

¼ cup (60 mL)
finely chopped speck

6 garlic cloves, chopped

1 small red onion,
finely chopped

1 beet, julienned

1 celery stalk, finely chopped

1 carrot, julienned

1 potato, diced

½ sweet potato, diced

½ small turnip, julienned

⅓ cup (80 mL) diced pumpkin

3 tablespoons (45 mL)
minced sun-dried tomatoes

2 bay leaves

¼ cup (60 mL) chopped basil

1 teaspoon (5 mL) chopped
oregano

Sea salt and freshly
cracked pepper

4 cups (1 L) boiling water

1½ cups (375 mL) chopped
fresh tomatoes

½ cup (125 mL) green beans

1 small zucchini, julienned

Grated Parmesan cheese

—

HEAT 2 tbsp (30 mL) oil in a large saucepan over medium heat. Fry speck, garlic and onion for 3 minutes.

ADD all remaining ingredients except water, fresh tomatoes, beans and zucchini. Season and cook for 7 minutes.

ADD boiling water and fresh tomatoes; simmer until vegetables are tender.

ADD beans and zucchini and simmer for 5 minutes. Remove bay leaves. Garnish with Parmesan and a drizzle of the remaining oil just before serving.

×

—
Variation

For a classic Italian minestrone, you can leave out the beets and add cooked white beans and cooked short pasta.

Andalusian Lentil Soup with Apricots

—

2 tablespoons (30 mL) olive oil

1 onion, chopped

4 garlic cloves, chopped

1 tablespoon (15 mL) ground cumin + 1 teaspoon (5 mL) smoked paprika + ½ teaspoon (2 mL) cinnamon + ¼ teaspoon (1 mL) chili powder

¾ cup (180 mL) crushed tomatoes (fresh or canned)

½ cup (125 mL) red lentils

12 dried apricots, minced

1 stalk celery, minced

½ sweet red pepper, julienned

Juice of 1 lemon

Leaves from 2 thyme sprigs

6 cups (1.5 L) boiling water

Sea salt and freshly cracked pepper

2 tablespoons (30 mL) chopped parsley

—

HEAT oil in a large saucepan over medium heat. Cook onion, garlic, and spices for 5 minutes.

ADD remaining ingredients except parsley. Simmer for 20 minutes or until lentils are cooked. Stir occasionally and add water as needed.

SEASON and garnish with parsley.

×

Borscht of Jerusalem Artichokes

—

2 tablespoons (30 mL) olive oil

1 tablespoon (15 mL) butter

1 tablespoon (15 mL) caraway seeds
+ 1 tablespoon (15 mL) cumin seeds + 5 whole cloves

3 garlic cloves, chopped

2 medium onions, chopped

½ leek, minced

4 to 5 cups (1 to 1.25 L) boiling water

½ cup (125 mL) crushed tomatoes (fresh or canned)

¾ cup (180 mL) peeled Jerusalem artichokes cut into pieces

2 cups (500 mL) shredded red cabbage

1 tablespoon (15 mL) balsamic vinegar

1½ teaspoons (7 mL) cane sugar

Sea salt and freshly cracked pepper

2 tablespoons (30 mL) chopped dill

Sour cream

—

HEAT oil and butter in a medium saucepan over medium heat. Cook spices, garlic, onions and leek for 10 minutes, moistening with 1 tbsp (15 mL) water if necessary.

STIR in remaining ingredients except dill and sour cream. Simmer, covered, over low heat for 20 minutes or until Jerusalem artichokes are tender. Season.

GARNISH with dill and sour cream just before serving.

×

Roasted Root Vegetable Soup

—

4 parsnips, cut into large chunks

2 carrots, cut into large chunks

1 medium onion, quartered

4 tomatoes, quartered

3 garlic cloves, peeled

3 tablespoons (45 mL) olive oil

1 tablespoon (15 mL) ground cumin + 1 tablespoon (15 mL) turmeric + 1 tablespoon (15 mL) crushed coriander seeds + 1 teaspoon (5 mL) mustard seeds

3 cups (750 mL) boiling water

Juice of ½ lemon

Sea salt and freshly cracked pepper

¼ cup (60 mL) chopped parsley

—

PREHEAT oven to 400°F (200°C).

TOSS vegetables with oil and spices.

PLACE vegetables in a roasting pan with 1 cup (250 mL) boiling water. Cover with foil and bake for 15 minutes.

REMOVE foil and reduce oven temperature to 350°F (180°C). Continue cooking for 15 minutes or until vegetables are tender.

PURÉE in a blender with 2 cups (500 mL) boiling water. Stir in lemon juice and season.

GARNISH with parsley just before serving.

×

Onion Soup with Guinness and Tarragon

—

1 tablespoon (15 mL) olive oil

1 tablespoon (15 mL) butter

½ teaspoon (2 mL) nutmeg + ½ teaspoon (2 mL) cumin seeds + ½ teaspoon (2 mL) ground allspice

2 onions, finely chopped

1 leek, finely chopped

3 cups (750 mL) boiling water

Leaves from 2 thyme sprigs

½ teaspoon (2 mL) grainy mustard

4 cloves garlic confit (see below)

1 cup (250 mL) Guinness or other dark stout

Sea salt and freshly cracked pepper

¼ cup (60 mL) chopped tarragon

6 slices toast

2 cups (500 mL) grated sharp Cheddar cheese

—

Garlic Confit

Wrap a head of garlic drizzled with olive oil in foil, and bake for 30 minutes at 400°F (200°C). Extract garlic cloves from the skin and mash into a paste.

The cloves that are not being used can be frozen. Garlic confit is perfect for vegetable soups, sauces or mayonnaise.

—

HEAT oil and butter in a large saucepan over medium heat. Add spices, onions and leek; cook for 10 minutes or until onion caramelizes, moistening with 1 tbsp (15 mL) water if required.

STIR in boiling water, thyme, mustard and garlic confit. Simmer for 10 minutes.

ADD stout and cook another 5 minutes to heat through. Season.

PREHEAT broiler. Pour soup into ovenproof bowls. Garnish each bowl with tarragon. Place a slice of toast on each bowl and top with cheese. Broil.

×

Saint-Germain Soup with Mint

—

1 tablespoon (15 mL) butter or olive oil

1 onion, finely chopped

1 lb (500 g) frozen peas

2 mint sprigs, plus leaves for garnish

2 cups (500 mL) boiling water

⅓ cup (80 mL) 35% cream (optional)

Sea salt and freshly cracked pepper

—

Variations

You can replace the mint with tarragon.

Do like the English: drain pea mixture and purée into a mash. Serve with lamb.

—

HEAT butter in a saucepan over medium heat. Add onion and cook for 5 minutes or until softened.

ADD peas, mint and water. Bring to a boil, reduce heat and simmer, covered, for 10 minutes. Remove mint.

PURÉE in a blender, without adding all the cooking liquid. Add cream, if desired, or more cooking liquid to achieve desired consistency.

SEASON. Garnish with mint leaves just before serving.

×

St. Patrick Chickpea Soup

—

1 tablespoon (15 mL) butter

2 tablespoons (30 mL) olive oil

1 medium onion, chopped

½ teaspoon (2 mL) nutmeg + 1 tablespoon (15 mL) ground cumin

2 large potatoes, peeled and cubed

4 cups (1 L) boiling water

1 tablespoon (15 mL) balsamic vinegar

6 oz (170 g) grated old Cheddar cheese

6 tablespoons (90 mL) 35% cream

1 leek, finely chopped

Leaves from 1 thyme sprig

Sea salt and freshly cracked pepper

1 cup (250 mL) cooked chickpeas

¼ cup (60 mL) chopped parsley

—

HEAT butter and oil in a large saucepan over medium heat. Cook onion with spices for 5 minutes or until onion has softened.

ADD potatoes, boiling water and vinegar. Simmer for 10 minutes or until potatoes are tender.

STIR in cheese and cream, then purée in a blender.

ADD leeks and thyme. Simmer over low heat for 10 minutes, stirring occasionally. Season.

ADD the chickpeas and parsley. Reheat for a few minutes.

×

Lemongrass Parmentier or Vichyssoise

—

2 tablespoons (30 mL) butter

3 garlic cloves, chopped

2 onions, chopped

2 leeks, thinly sliced

2 stalks lemongrass, bruised using the back of a knife

4 kaffir lime leaves (or juice of 2 limes)

1 lb (500 g) potatoes, peeled and cut into large chunks

6 cups (1.5 L) boiling water

Sea salt and freshly cracked pepper

½ cup (125 mL) 35% cream

8 chives, finely chopped

—

Variation

For a classic vichyssoise, just replace the lemongrass and lime leaves with 2 bay leaves.

—

MELT butter in a large saucepan over medium heat. Cook garlic, onions, leeks, lemongrass and lime leaves for 10 minutes. If mixture starts to dry, moisten with 1 tbsp (15 mL) water.

ADD potatoes and boiling water. Season with salt. Bring to a boil, then reduce heat and simmer for 15 minutes or until potatoes are tender.

POUR in cream. Remove lemongrass and lime leaves. Season. Purée in a blender.

GARNISH soup with chives. Soup can be served hot as a parmentier or cold as a vichyssoise.

×

Deep South Corn and Cabbage Soup

—

2 tablespoons (30 mL) olive oil

1 tablespoon (15 mL) butter

2 medium onions, finely chopped

6 garlic cloves, chopped

1 tablespoon (15 mL) cumin seeds + 1 teaspoon (5 mL) ground allspice + 1 teaspoon (5 mL) ground ginger + ½ teaspoon (2 mL) paprika + ½ teaspoon (2 mL) cayenne + ¼ teaspoon (1 mL) turmeric

5 cups (1.25 L) boiling water

1½ cups (375 mL) corn kernels (frozen or fresh, see p. 152)

½ cup (125 mL) yellow split peas

1 carrot, diced

1 cup (250 mL) shredded green cabbage

1 teaspoon (5 mL) white wine vinegar

6 tablespoons (90 mL) 35% cream

Sea salt and freshly cracked pepper

—

HEAT oil and butter in a large saucepan over medium-high heat. Sauté onions, garlic and spices for 2 to 5 minutes.

ADD remaining ingredients except cream. Simmer, covered, for 45 minutes or until split peas are tender.

PURÉE half of the soup in a food processor. Stir in cream.

RETURN everything to the saucepan, season and simmer for another 5 minutes to warm through.

×

Corn Chowder with Lemongrass

—

2 tablespoons (30 mL)
olive oil

1 tablespoon (15 mL) butter

1 small red onion,
finely chopped

1 leek, finely chopped

4 garlic cloves, chopped

1 tablespoon (15 mL)
ground coriander

½ teaspoon (2 mL) turmeric

3 cups (750 mL)
boiling water

1 cup (250 mL) milk

1 large potato,
peeled and diced

1½ cups (375 mL) corn
kernels (frozen or fresh,
see p. 152)

1 celery stalk,
finely chopped

1 stalk lemongrass,
white part only, bruised
using the back of a knife

½ teaspoon (2 mL)
red pepper flakes

3 tablespoons (45 mL)
chopped cilantro

10 spinach leaves, chopped

⅓ cup (80 mL) 35% cream

Sea salt and freshly
cracked pepper

—

HEAT oil and butter in a saucepan over medium heat. Cook onion, leek and garlic with coriander and turmeric for 10 minutes. If mixture starts to dry, moisten with 1 tbsp (15 mL) water.

ADD remaining ingredients except cilantro, spinach and cream. Simmer, covered, for 15 minutes or until potato is tender.

STIR in spinach, cilantro and cream. Season. Simmer for another 5 minutes.

REMOVE lemongrass before serving.

×

Yucatán Yucca, Corn and Sweet Potato Soup

—

2 tablespoons (30 mL) vegetable oil

1 large onion, finely chopped

2 tablespoons (30 mL) ground coriander

¼ teaspoon (1 mL) chili powder

1½ cups (375 mL) cubed yucca

1 cup (250 mL) corn kernels (frozen or fresh, see p. 152)

5 cups (1.25 L) boiling water

1½ cups (375 mL) cubed sweet potato

6 tablespoons (90 mL) cream

¼ cup (60 mL) yogurt

2 tablespoons (30 mL) chopped cilantro

Freshly cracked pepper

—

HEAT oil in a large saucepan over medium heat. Cook onion with coriander and chili powder for 5 minutes.

ADD yucca, corn and boiling water. Cook, covered, for 10 to 15 minutes or until yucca is tender.

STIR in sweet potato, cream, yogurt and half the cilantro. Simmer for 10 minutes or until sweet potato is tender. Season.

GARNISH with remaining cilantro just before serving.

×

Black Bean Peanut Mole Soup

—

2 tablespoons (30 mL) olive oil

1 tablespoon (15 mL) ground cumin + 2 tablespoons (30 mL) ground coriander + 1 teaspoon (5 mL) red pepper flakes

2 medium onions, finely chopped

6 garlic cloves, chopped

½ sweet red pepper, julienned

3 large tomatoes, chopped

4 cups (1 L) boiling water

1 tablespoon (15 mL) cocoa powder

1 tablespoon (15 mL) cane sugar (or less depending on bitterness of the cocoa)

5 teaspoons (25 mL) natural peanut butter

Sea salt and freshly cracked pepper

2 cups (500 mL) cooked black beans

¼ cup (60 mL) chopped cilantro

—

HEAT oil in a large saucepan over medium heat. Cook spices, onions and garlic for 2 minutes or until fragrant.

ADD remaining ingredients except black beans and cilantro. Simmer, covered, for 25 minutes. Season.

STIR in black beans and cilantro. Cook for 5 minutes to warm through.

×

Brazilian Bean Soup with Tomato

—

¼ cup (60 mL) olive oil

1 red onion, finely chopped

1 tablespoon (15 mL) curry powder + 3 tablespoons (45 mL) ground coriander

2 large sweet potatoes, peeled and diced

2 cups (500 mL) crushed tomatoes (fresh or canned)

5 cups (1.25 L) boiling water

2 tablespoons (30 mL) balsamic vinegar

Sea salt and freshly cracked pepper

2 cups (500 mL) cooked red kidney beans

¼ cup (60 mL) chopped cilantro

—

HEAT oil in a large saucepan over medium-high heat. Add onion, curry powder and ground coriander; sauté 5 minutes.

ADD sweet potatoes, tomatoes, boiling water and vinegar. Simmer for 10 minutes or until sweet potatoes are cooked. Season.

STIR in kidney beans and chopped cilantro. Cook for 5 minutes to warm through.

×

Louisiana Vegetable Soup

—

2 tablespoons (30 mL) olive oil

½ leek, finely chopped

1 medium onion, finely chopped

4 garlic cloves, chopped

2 tablespoons (30 mL) grated fresh ginger

1 tablespoon (15 mL) ground cumin + 1 teaspoon (5 mL) paprika + 1 teaspoon (5 mL) ground allspice + ½ teaspoon (2 mL) cayenne + ½ teaspoon (2 mL) cinnamon

5 cups (1.25 L) boiling water

1 cup (250 mL) crushed tomatoes (fresh or canned)

½ sweet red pepper, julienned

1 carrot, julienned

1 celery stalk, finely chopped

1 large sweet potato, cubed

¾ cup (180 mL) corn kernels (frozen or fresh, see p. 152)

Leaves from 2 thyme sprigs

1 bay leaf

1 tablespoon (15 mL) sherry vinegar

Sea salt and freshly cracked pepper

6 okra, julienned

1 cup (250 mL) shredded green cabbage

½ cup (125 mL) cooked red kidney beans

2 tablespoons (30 mL) chopped parsley

—

HEAT oil in a large saucepan over medium heat. Cook leek, onion, garlic, ginger and spices for 5 to 10 minutes, until onion is softened, moistening if necessary with 1 tbsp (15 mL) water.

ADD remaining ingredients, except okra, cabbage, beans and parsley. Season. Simmer for 30 minutes or until vegetables are tender.

STIR in remaining ingredients and simmer another 5 minutes to heat through. Remove bay leaf and serve.

×

Jamaican Sweet Potato and Bean Soup

---

2 tablespoons (30 mL) olive oil

1 onion, finely chopped

4 garlic cloves, chopped

1 tablespoon (15 mL) grated fresh ginger

1 tablespoon (15 mL) ground cumin + 1 teaspoon (5 mL) ground allspice + ½ teaspoon (2 mL) cayenne + ¼ teaspoon (1 mL) ground cloves + 1 cinnamon stick

1 sweet potato, peeled and diced

1 celery stalk, finely chopped

Leaves from 1 thyme sprig

Juice of ½ lime

3½ cups (875 mL) boiling water

Sea salt and freshly cracked pepper

2½ cups (625 mL) cooked red kidney beans

½ cup (125 mL) chopped cilantro

HEAT oil in a large saucepan over medium heat. Cook onion, garlic, ginger and spices for 5 to 10 minutes, until onion is softened.

ADD sweet potato, celery, thyme, lime juice and water. Season. Bring to a boil, then reduce heat and simmer, covered, for 25 minutes or until vegetables are tender.

STIR in kidney beans and chopped cilantro. Simmer for another 5 minutes to heat through.

×

Summer Mulligatawny Soup with Tomato and Apple

—

3 tablespoons (45 mL) currants

3 cups (750 mL) brewed Assam black tea

¼ cup (60 mL) olive oil

3 garlic cloves, chopped

1 medium onion, finely chopped

2 celery stalks, finely chopped

4 tomatoes, chopped

½ cup (125 mL) unsweetened shredded coconut

1 tablespoon (15 mL) curry powder

Sea salt and freshly cracked pepper

1 tablespoon (15 mL) butter

2 apples (McIntosh or Cortland), finely chopped

—

SOAK currants in brewed tea for 10 minutes or until plumped. Drain currants, reserving tea, and set both aside.

HEAT oil in a saucepan over medium heat. Cook garlic, onion and celery for 3 minutes or until fragrant.

ADD tomatoes, coconut, curry powder and reserved tea. Bring to a boil, then reduce heat to low and simmer for 20 to 25 minutes or until celery is tender.

PURÉE in a blender. Season.

HEAT butter in a large skillet over medium heat. Add apples and cook for 10 minutes or until caramelized.

STIR apples and currants into soup just before serving.

×

Winter Mulligatawny Soup with Lentils and Sweet Potatoes

—

¼ cup (60 mL) slivered almonds

¼ cup (60 mL) olive oil

2 medium onions, finely chopped

½ sweet red pepper, julienned

2 inches (5 cm) fresh ginger, peeled and cut into large chunks

1 teaspoon (5 mL) ground cardamom + 1 teaspoon (5 mL) ground cumin + 1 teaspoon (5 mL) ground coriander + 1 teaspoon (5 mL) curry powder + ½ teaspoon (2 mL) red pepper flakes

Sea salt and freshly cracked pepper

5 cups (1.25 L) boiling water

⅓ cup (80 mL) brown lentils

1 large sweet potato, peeled and diced

Juice of 1 lemon

3 tablespoons (45 mL) yogurt

1 Granny Smith apple, unpeeled and finely chopped

3 tablespoons (45 mL) chopped cilantro

—

TOAST almonds in a dry skillet until golden. Reserve.

HEAT oil in a large saucepan over medium heat. Cook onions, red pepper, ginger and spices for 5 minutes or until softened. Season.

STIR in boiling water and lentils. Cook, covered, for 25 minutes or until lentils are tender. Add more water if mixture becomes too dry.

ADD sweet potato and lemon juice. Reduce heat to low and simmer for 5 minutes or until sweet potato is almost tender.

STIR in yogurt, apple, chopped cilantro and toasted almonds. Simmer for another 5 minutes to heat through. Remove the ginger pieces before serving.

×

Oriental Chickpea Soup

2 tablespoons (30 mL) olive oil

5 garlic cloves, chopped

1 onion, finely chopped

1 teaspoon (5 mL) cumin seeds + ½ teaspoon (2 mL) red pepper flakes + ½ teaspoon (2 mL) turmeric

Leaves from 2 thyme sprigs

3 tomatoes, diced

1 celery stalk, finely chopped

3 cups (750 mL) boiling water

3 cups (750 mL) cooked chickpeas

1 cup (250 mL) cherry tomatoes (optional)

Sea salt and freshly cracked pepper

¼ cup (60 mL) chopped cilantro

HEAT oil in a saucepan over medium heat. Cook garlic, onion, spices and thyme for 10 minutes.

ADD tomatoes and cook for 2 minutes, until tomatoes soften.

STIR in celery and water. Bring to a boil, then reduce heat and simmer for 10 minutes.

ADD chickpeas and cherry tomatoes, if desired. Season. Simmer for another 5 minutes to heat through.

GARNISH with chopped cilantro just before serving.

×

Sweet-and-Sour Okra Soup

2 tablespoons (30 mL) olive oil

4 garlic cloves, chopped

1 teaspoon (5 mL) curry powder

1 teaspoon (5 mL) powdered galangal

6 tomatoes, diced

4 cups (1 L) boiling water

2 medium onions, finely chopped

½ sweet red pepper, julienned

6 okra, julienned

1 tablespoon (15 mL) cane sugar

Juice of 1 lemon and 1 lime

Sea salt and freshly cracked pepper

Galangal

This rhizome looks and tastes a lot like ginger, but it is less pungent.

HEAT 1 tbsp (15 mL) oil in a large saucepan over medium heat. Cook garlic, curry powder and galangal for 1 to 2 minutes or until fragrant.

STIR in tomatoes and boiling water. Simmer for 10 minutes. Purée using an immersion blender.

HEAT remaining 1 tbsp (15 mL) oil in a large skillet over medium heat. Sauté onions and red pepper for 5 minutes or until softened. Add to soup.

STIR in remaining ingredients. Simmer for 5 minutes to heat through. Season.

Dhal Soup

—

¼ cup (60 mL) olive oil

2 tablespoons (30 mL) butter

1 tablespoon (15 mL) cumin seeds + 1 tablespoon (15 mL) coriander seeds + 1 teaspoon fenugreek seeds + 1 teaspoon (5 mL) black mustard seeds + ½ teaspoon (2 mL) turmeric

1 onion, finely chopped

2 inches (5 cm) fresh ginger, peeled and cut into large chunks

Sea salt and freshly cracked pepper

6 cups (1.5 L) boiling water

1 cup (250 mL) red lentils or dried mung beans

Red pepper flakes

3 tablespoons (45 mL) chopped cilantro

—

Black mustard seeds

Indian cuisine favours this type of mustard, which has a stronger flavour than yellow mustard seeds.

—

HEAT oil and butter in a large saucepan over medium-high heat. Add spices, onion and ginger. Season. Sauté for 5 minutes or until onion is softened.

STIR in water and lentils. Simmer, covered, for 15 minutes or until lentils are cooked (40 minutes if using mung beans). Stir occasionally and add water as needed. Remove ginger pieces.

SEASON with pepper flakes and garnish with chopped cilantro.

×

Korean Cabbage and Edamame Soup

4 cups (1 L) water

5 dried shiitake mushrooms

2 tablespoons (30 mL) olive oil

1 teaspoon (5 mL) toasted sesame oil

4 garlic cloves, chopped

2 inches (5 cm) fresh ginger, peeled and cut into large chunks

2 green onions, chopped

½ sweet red pepper, finely chopped

1 celery stalk, julienned

1 small carrot, julienned

4 tomatoes, diced

2 tablespoons (30 mL) tamari

1 tablespoon (15 mL) rice vinegar

1½ cups (375 mL) sliced Chinese cabbage or bok choy

6 tablespoons (90 mL) chopped cilantro

½ cup (125 mL) shelled edamame

Edamame

Edamame are fresh soybeans still in their pods. They are found in the frozen food aisle of grocery stores and are sold shelled or unshelled (and preferably organic). To cook, simply steam edamame for 3 minutes.

BOIL the water in a small saucepan. Add shiitakes, cover and simmer for 10 minutes or until caps are tender. Drain mushrooms, reserving cooking water. finely chop the caps and discard stems. Set aside.

HEAT oils in a large saucepan over medium-high heat. Sauté garlic, ginger, green onions, red pepper, celery and carrot for 5 minutes.

ADD reserved mushrooms, tomatoes, tamari, vinegar and cooking water. Simmer for a few minutes to heat through.

STIR in cabbage and chopped cilantro. Cook for 3 minutes or until cabbage is tender-crisp.

ADD edamame at the very end of cooking so they retain their colour and tenderness. Remove ginger pieces before serving.

×

Thai Pumpkin and Spinach Soup

—

Laksa Paste

1 tablespoon (15 mL) olive oil

4 green onions, finely chopped

2 garlic cloves, chopped

2 teaspoons (10 mL) grated fresh ginger

2 small chilies, seeded and finely chopped

1 tablespoon (15 mL) finely chopped lemongrass (white part only)

½ teaspoon (2 mL) turmeric + 2 teaspoons (10 mL) ground cumin + 1 teaspoon (5 mL) ground coriander

1 tablespoon (15 mL) cane sugar

—

Soup

1 butternut squash, cut into large chunks

4 cups (1 L) boiling water

1 can (5 oz/140 mL) coconut milk

6 cups (1.5 L) coarsely chopped spinach

Leaves from ½ bunch basil

1 cup (250 mL) bean sprouts

—

COMBINE ingredients for laksa paste in a large saucepan. Sauté over medium-high heat for 3 minutes.

STIR in squash and sauté for 1 minute to coat in laksa paste.

POUR in water and coconut milk. Bring to a boil, then reduce heat and simmer for 5 minutes or until squash is tender.

STIR in spinach. Garnish with basil leaves and bean sprouts just before serving.

×

Asian Mushroom Soup

—

6 cups (1.5 L) boiling water

5 dried shiitake mushrooms

2 tablespoons (30 mL) olive oil

6 garlic cloves, chopped

2 tablespoons (30 mL) grated fresh ginger

2 portobello mushrooms, stems removed, chopped

1 cup (250 mL) sliced oyster mushrooms

¼ cup (60 mL) brandy

2 tablespoons (30 mL) sherry vinegar

1 tablespoon (15 mL) tamari

2 green onions, thinly sliced

Sea salt

1 cup (250 mL) quartered baby bok choy

15 basil leaves, finely chopped

9 oz (255 g) cooked vermicelli noodles (optional)

—

BOIL the water in a saucepan. Add shiitakes, cover and simmer for 10 minutes or until caps are tender.

DRAIN mushrooms, reserving cooking water. Chop the caps and discard stems. Set aside.

HEAT oil in a large saucepan over medium-high heat. Sauté garlic, ginger, portobellos and oyster mushrooms for 7 to 10 minutes or until tender.

ADD cooking water, brandy, vinegar, tamari, green onions and shiitakes. Add salt if necessary. Bring to a boil, then remove from heat and add bok choy and basil.

PLACE a serving of vermicelli, if desired, in each bowl before adding hot soup.

×

Malaysian Eggplant Soup with Lentils

—

1 medium eggplant, diced

4 tablespoons (60 mL) olive oil

4 garlic cloves, chopped

1 onion, finely chopped

2 tablespoons (30 mL) grated fresh ginger

½ teaspoon (2 mL) finely chopped bird's eye chili

1 teaspoon (5 mL) fennel seeds + 1 teaspoon (5 mL) ground cloves + 1 teaspoon (5 mL) ground cardamom

4 tomatoes, diced

½ cup (125 mL) red lentils

4 cups (1 L) boiling water

Sea salt

3 tablespoons (45 mL) chopped cilantro

2 tablespoons (30 mL) chopped mint

—

PREHEAT oven to 400°F (200°C).

PLACE eggplant on a parchment-lined baking sheet. Brush with 2 tbsp (30 mL) oil. Bake for 5 to 10 minutes or until eggplant is roasted. Reserve.

HEAT remaining 2 tbsp (30 mL) oil in a saucepan over medium-high heat. Sauté garlic, onion, ginger, chili and spices for 5 minutes. Add tomatoes and let stew for 2 minutes.

ADD lentils, roasted eggplant and water. Season with salt. Reduce heat to low and simmer, covered, for 15 to 20 minutes, stirring occasionally, until lentils are cooked. Add water as needed.

STIR in chopped cilantro and mint before serving.

×

Indonesian Green Bean Soup

—

1 teaspoon (5 mL) toasted sesame oil

2 tablespoons (30 mL) olive oil

1 tablespoon (15 mL) butter

2 onions, finely chopped

2 inches (5 cm) fresh ginger, peeled and cut into large chunks

½ teaspoon (2 mL) finely chopped bird's eye chili

1 tablespoon (15 mL) ground cardamom
+ 1 tablespoon (15 mL) cumin seeds + 1 tablespoon (15 mL) ground coriander + 1 teaspoon (5 mL) black mustard seeds

2 potatoes, peeled and cut into large cubes

3 cups (750 mL) boiling water

1 tablespoon (15 mL) tamari

Juice of 1 lime

Sea salt

½ cup (125 mL) green beans, cut into pieces

¼ cup (60 mL) chopped cilantro

¼ cup (60 mL) 35% cream

—

HEAT oils and butter in a large saucepan over medium heat. Cook onions, ginger, chili and spices for 10 minutes or until onion is softened.

STIR in potatoes, water, tamari and lime juice. Season with salt. Reduce heat and simmer, covered, for 10 minutes or until potatoes are tender.

ADD green beans, chopped cilantro and cream. Simmer for another 2 minutes, until beans are tender-crisp. Remove ginger pieces before serving.

×

Clam Chowder

—

1 lb (500 g) whole clams, scrubbed clean

½ cup (125 mL) white wine

3 tablespoons (45 mL) butter

2 small onions, finely chopped

3 celery stalks, finely chopped

2 cups (500 mL) new potatoes, cut into 2 or 3 pieces

2 cups (500 mL) boiling water

Leaves from 7 thyme sprigs

2 bay leaves

1 cup (250 mL) corn kernels (frozen or fresh, see p. 152)

½ cup (125 mL) 35% cream

Sea salt and freshly cracked pepper

Chopped chives

Smoked paprika

—

Manhattan-Style Chowder

Omit cream and corn. Add 1½ cups (375 mL) chopped tomatoes when cooking the potatoes.

PLACE clams in a large saucepan with the wine, cover and bring to boil over high heat. Boil for 5 minutes, until clamshells open.

DISCARD any clams that have not opened. Remove clams from shells and reserve cooking liquid.

MELT butter in the same saucepan over medium heat. Cook onions and celery for 5 minutes, until softened but not browning.

ADD potatoes, water, thyme and bay leaves. Cook for 10 to 15 minutes or until potatoes are just tender.

STIR in corn, clams and their cooking liquid; simmer for 5 minutes. Remove bay leaves.

POUR in cream and season. Serve chowder garnished with chives and a pinch of paprika.

×

Thai Shrimp Soup

—

3 tablespoons (45 mL) green curry paste (see below)

1 cup (250 mL) baby corn

4 bok choy, quartered

1 lb (500 g) large shrimp, peeled

1⅔ cups (400 mL) coconut milk

2 cups (500 mL) boiling water

1 cup (250 mL) snow peas, julienned lengthwise

2 tablespoons (30 mL) fish sauce

1 tablespoon (15 mL) cane sugar

Juice of 1 lime

4 cups (1 L) cooked basmati or jasmine rice

2 green onions, chopped

½ cup (125 mL) Thai or regular basil

—

Green Curry Paste

Combine 1 tablespoon (15 mL) ground cumin, 2 tablespoons (30 mL) ground coriander, 2 chopped lemongrass stalks (white part only), 4 green onions, 4 garlic cloves, 2 green chilies, seeded, 1 inch (2.5 cm) peeled fresh ginger, 1 cup (250 mL) cilantro, 2 tablespoons (30 mL) canola oil and 2 tablespoons (30 mL) water in a blender. Blend to obtain a thick, smooth paste. Season with salt. Refrigerate for up to a week, or freeze.

HEAT curry paste in a wok over high heat, stirring constantly. Add baby corn and bok choy and cook for 2 minutes.

ADD shrimp, coconut milk and water. Reduce heat to low and simmer until shrimp turn pink, about 3 minutes.

STIR in snow peas, fish sauce, sugar and lime juice. Cook for a few minutes to heat through.

LADLE soup into large bowls. Serve with a good scoop of rice, garnished with green onion and basil leaves.

×

Fish Soup with Tarragon

—

2 tablespoons (30 mL) olive oil

1 onion, finely chopped

1 leek, julienned

1 small fennel bulb, julienned

3 tomatoes, diced

¼ cup (60 mL) pastis or white wine

4 cups (1 L) boiling water

1 lb (500 g) skinless fresh cod fillet, cut into pieces

2 tablespoons (30 mL) chopped tarragon

Juice of 1 lime or ½ orange

Sea salt and freshly cracked pepper

4 slices crusty bread, toasted

—

HEAT oil in a saucepan over medium heat. Cook onion, leek and fennel for a few minutes, until golden.

ADD tomatoes and cook for 2 minutes. Deglaze with pastis and cook for several minutes to reduce slightly.

POUR in boiling water. Add cod, tarragon and lime juice. Simmer for 3 to 4 minutes or until cod is cooked through. Season.

SERVE fish soup with toast.

×

Indonesian Chicken Soup

—

1 tablespoon (15 mL)
sesame oil

2 dried red chili peppers

1 small garlic clove, crushed

4 green onions, chopped

¾ lb (375 g) boneless,
skinless chicken,
cut into pieces

4 cups (1 L) chicken or
turkey stock (p. 40)

1½ cups (375 mL)
coconut milk

2 tablespoons (30 mL)
soy sauce

1 cup (250 mL) cooked
egg noodles

1 cup (250 mL) bean sprouts

3 cups (750 mL) coarsely
chopped spinach or
bok choy

1 cup (250 mL)
chopped cilantro

—

HEAT sesame oil in a saucepan over medium-high heat. Sauté chilies, garlic and green onions for 5 minutes.

ADD chicken, stock, coconut milk and soy sauce. Reduce heat to low and simmer for 10 minutes or until chicken is cooked through.

DIVIDE cooked noodles among 4 large bowls. Add bean sprouts and spinach. Pour soup on top and garnish each bowl with chopped cilantro.

×

Thai Turkey Soup

—

2 tablespoons (30 mL) olive oil

1 boneless, skinless turkey breast, chopped

1 large onion, finely chopped

4 garlic cloves, chopped

1 tablespoon (15 mL) ground coriander

1 tablespoon (15 mL) grated fresh ginger

5 cups (1.25 L) boiling water

1 stalk lemongrass, white part only, bruised using the back of a knife

Juice of 2 limes

2 celery stalks, finely chopped

2 carrots, thinly sliced

1 parsnip, thinly sliced

2 tablespoons (30 mL) tamari

1 teaspoon (5 mL) toasted sesame oil

½ bird's eye chili, finely chopped

3 tablespoons (15 mL) chopped cilantro

Sea salt and freshly ground pepper

—

HEAT oil in a large saucepan over medium-high heat. Add turkey pieces with onion and garlic and sauté for 5 minutes or until browned.

ADD coriander and ginger. Sauté for 2 minutes.

STIR in remaining ingredients. Reduce heat and simmer for 15 minutes or until turkey and vegetables are cooked. Adjust seasoning.

REMOVE lemongrass before serving.

Hungarian Chicken Soup

2 tablespoons (30 mL) olive oil

1 boneless, skinless chicken breast, cubed

1 small onion, minced

2 tablespoons (30 mL) grated fresh ginger

2 teaspoons (10 mL) paprika (not smoked) + 2 teaspoons (10 mL) cumin seeds + 1 teaspoon (5 mL) cinnamon

1 cup (250 mL) red lentils

⅔ cup (160 mL) crushed tomatoes (fresh or canned)

4 cups (1 L) boiling water

⅔ cup (160 mL) red wine

½ sweet potato, peeled and julienned

1 potato, peeled and julienned

½ sweet red pepper, roasted, peeled and diced

Sour cream

Sea salt

HEAT oil in a large saucepan over medium-high heat. Add chicken, onion, ginger and spices; cook for 5 to 10 minutes, until chicken is browned.

POUR in lentils, tomatoes, water and wine. Season with salt. Reduce heat and simmer for 10 minutes.

ADD sweet potato, potatoes and roasted pepper. Cook for another 15 minutes or until potatoes are tender.

SERVE with sour cream.

×

Chicken Tagine Soup

—

2 tablespoons (30 mL) olive oil

2 medium onions, chopped

2 teaspoons (10 mL) curry powder + 1 teaspoon (10 mL) turmeric + 1 teaspoon (10 mL) caraway seeds + 1 teaspoon (5 mL) ground coriander

1 dried chili + 1 whole clove + a pinch of saffron

4 boneless, skinless chicken thighs, cut into chunks

⅔ cup (160 mL) dried apricots, sliced

⅔ cup (160 mL) currants

4 cups (1 L) boiling water

Sea salt and freshly cracked pepper

1 cup (250 mL) chopped cilantro

—

HEAT oil in a large saucepan over medium heat. Cook onions for 3 minutes to soften.

ADD spices, chicken, apricots and currants. Cook over high heat for a few minutes, until chicken is golden.

ADD water. Reduce heat to low and simmer for 20 minutes or until chicken is cooked through. Adjust seasoning.

GARNISH each bowl with chopped cilantro just before serving.

×

Portuguese White Bean Soup with Chorizo

—

1 cup (250 mL)
sliced chorizo

5 garlic cloves

3 tablespoons (45 mL)
olive oil

2 onions, finely chopped

½ to 1 teaspoon (2 to 5 mL)
smoked paprika

4 cups (1 L) boiling water

2 cups (500 mL) cooked
white kidney beans

Sea salt and freshly
ground pepper

1 celery stalk,
finely chopped

Leaves from 2 thyme sprigs

½ cup (125 mL) shredded
collard greens or savoy
cabbage, blanched

—

PREHEAT oven to 400°F (200°C).

PLACE chorizo and garlic on a parchment-lined baking sheet. Brush garlic with 1 tbsp (15 mL) oil.

BAKE for 10 to 15 minutes or until chorizo and garlic are roasted. Reserve.

HEAT remaining 2 tbsp (30 mL) oil in a saucepan over medium-high heat. Sauté onions with paprika for 10 minutes or until onions are softened.

STIR in roasted garlic, water and 1 cup (250 mL) kidney beans. Simmer for 10 minutes. Purée in a blender. Season.

RETURN purée to saucepan and add celery, thyme, chorizo and remaining kidney beans. Simmer for a few minutes to heat through. Adjust seasoning.

SERVE soup garnished with blanched cabbage.

×

Harira with Lamb

—

2 tablespoons (30 mL) olive oil

3 onions, chopped

5 celery stalks, cut into ½-inch (1 cm) pieces

1 inch (2.5 cm) fresh ginger, peeled and grated

½ teaspoon (2 mL) saffron + 1 teaspoon (5 mL) turmeric + 1 teaspoon (5 mL) freshly cracked pepper + 1 cinnamon stick

2 lb (1 kg) boneless lamb leg or shoulder, cubed

1 cup (250 mL) lentils du Puy

1 cup (250 mL) dried chickpeas, soaked overnight

12 cups (3 L) boiling water

2 cups (500 mL) diced tomatoes

Zest and juice of ½ organic lemon

1 cup (250 mL) coarsely chopped cilantro

1 cup (250 mL) coarsely chopped parsley

Sea salt and freshly cracked pepper

1 cup (250 mL) cooked vermicelli noodles

—

HEAT oil in a large saucepan over medium-high heat. Working in batches if necessary so you don't crowd the pan, sauté onions, celery, ginger, spices and lamb for 5 minutes or until lamb is browned all over.

STIR in lentils, chickpeas and water. Reduce heat to low and simmer, uncovered, for 40 minutes or until chickpeas are tender.

ADD tomatoes, lemon zest and lemon juice. Cook for 5 minutes to heat through.

STIR in cilantro and parsley. Cook for 2 minutes to meld flavours. Season.

DIVIDE vermicelli among bowls. Ladle harira over top.

×

Beef Borscht

—

3 tablespoons (45 mL) olive oil

1 cup (250 mL) cubed stewing beef

1 tablespoon (15 mL) butter

1 onion, finely chopped

2 tablespoons (30 mL) chopped garlic

½ teaspoon (2 mL) ground anise + ½ teaspoon (2 mL) cumin seeds + ½ teaspoon (2 mL) caraway seeds

3 whole cloves + 1 bay leaf

5 cups (1.25 L) boiling water

1 celery stalk, finely chopped

1½ beets, peeled and diced

½ tomato, diced

¼ cup (60 mL) finely chopped fennel

½ cup (125 mL) shredded green cabbage

1 tablespoon (15 mL) balsamic vinegar

Sea salt and freshly cracked pepper

Sour cream

Chopped dill

—

HEAT 1 tbsp (15 mL) oil in a large saucepan over high heat. Add beef and brown on all sides. Transfer beef to a bowl along with cooking juices. Reserve.

HEAT remaining 2 tbsp (30 mL) oil and butter over medium-high heat in same pan. Sauté onion and garlic with the spices until browned.

STIR in remaining ingredients except sour cream and dill. Reduce heat and simmer, covered, for 25 minutes. Season.

ADD beef and its juices. Simmer for another 25 minutes or until beets are cooked through and beef is tender. Adjust seasoning and add water as needed. Remove bay leaf.

GARNISH borscht with sour cream and chopped dill.

×

Beef and Cabbage Soup

—

2 tablespoons (30 mL) olive oil

1 onion, finely chopped

1 lb (500 g) beef back ribs

4 tomatoes, diced

Leaves from 2 thyme sprigs

5 cups (1.25 L) boiling water

1 small turnip, cubed

1 tablespoon (15 mL) butter

2 cups (500 mL) shredded green cabbage

Sea salt and freshly cracked pepper

—

HEAT oil in a saucepan over high heat. Add onion and ribs, rotating meat to brown on all sides.

ADD tomatoes, thyme and water. Reduce heat and simmer, covered, for 45 minutes.

STIR in remaining ingredients and cook for 15 minutes or until vegetables are tender. Season.

REMOVE ribs and shred meat. Serve with vegetables and broth.

×

② Salads

& AUX HERB[...]

OCTOBER FEST (ve[...]
...a muscade), fèves no[...]

LA VEUVE BLANCHE

...e, céleri-rave, panais

✳ ✳ ✳ ✳ ✳

SAL[...]

Carrot Salad

—

1 lb (500 g) carrots

3 shallots or 1 small red onion, thinly sliced

1 teaspoon (5 mL) cumin seeds

⅓ cup (80 mL) olive oil

Zest and juice of 1 organic lemon

1 teaspoon (5 mL) grated fresh ginger

1 cup (250 mL) chopped mint

1 cup (250 mL) chopped cilantro

1 teaspoon (5 mL) sesame seeds

—

SHAVE carrots into long strips using a vegetable peeler. Place carrots and shallots in a bowl.

HEAT cumin seeds in a dry skillet over medium heat for 1 minute.

WHISK together oil, lemon zest and lemon juice, ginger and toasted cumin seeds.

POUR dressing over carrots and toss to combine. Add mint, cilantro and sesame seeds just before serving.

×

Serves 4

Red Cabbage and Apple Coleslaw

—

1 small red cabbage (about 10 oz/300 g)

3 carrots

2 apples

1 teaspoon (5 mL) dry mustard

2 tablespoons (30 mL) sherry or cider vinegar

Sea salt and freshly cracked pepper

6 tablespoons (60 mL) olive oil

—

SHRED cabbage, carrots and apples. Transfer to a large bowl.

MIX mustard and vinegar in a small bowl. Season. Slowly pour in oil while whisking to emulsify.

TOSS dressing with cabbage mixture. Adjust seasoning.

REFRIGERATE for 2 hours before serving.

×

Curried Tomato and Peach Salad

—

¼ cup (60 mL) olive oil

Juice of 1 lemon

½ teaspoon (2 mL)
curry powder

A pinch of sea salt

½ cup (125 mL) chopped
flat-leaf parsley

½ cup (125 mL) chopped
cilantro or basil

2 vine tomatoes, quartered

2 peaches, pitted
and quartered

—

Watermelon Salad
with Curry

Replace the tomatoes
and peaches with cubed
watermelon, and the lemon
juice with lime juice.

—

COMBINE oil, lemon juice, curry powder, salt and herbs in a small bowl and mix well.

DIVIDE tomatoes and peaches among 4 individual bowls. Drizzle with dressing and serve.

×

Blood Orange Salad with Basil

—

Vinaigrette

¼ cup (60 mL) olive oil

1 tablespoon (15 mL)
white balsamic vinegar

1 tablespoon (15 mL)
lime juice

A pinch of red pepper flakes
(optional)

—

Salad

4 blood oranges,
peeled and sliced

1 small red onion,
thinly sliced

6 cups (1.5 L) baby spinach

1 cup (250 mL)
chopped basil

½ cup (125 mL)
dried cranberries

½ cup (125 mL)
pumpkin seeds

—

WHISK vinaigrette ingredients in a large bowl.

ADD all salad ingredients except cranberries and pumpkin seeds. Toss well to combine.

DIVIDE salad among plates. Garnish with cranberries and pumpkin seeds.

×

Serves 4

Mâche Salad with Pear

—

Juice of 1 lemon
(or 1 tablespoon/15 mL
white balsamic vinegar)

2 tablespoons (30 mL)
olive oil + 1 tablespoon
(15 mL) hazelnut oil

Sea salt and freshly
cracked pepper

4 cups (1 L) mâche
or purslane

2 pears, cored and
thinly sliced

4 oz (120 g)
Comté cheese, sliced

1 cup (250 mL) blackberries

—

WHISK lemon juice with oils. Season.

PLACE the mâche and pears in a serving bowl. Pour over desired amount of vinaigrette and toss gently.

GARNISH with blackberries and cheese.

×

Serves 4

Zucchini Carpaccio

—

4 medium zucchini
(2 yellow, 2 green)

Sea salt and freshly
cracked pepper

2 tablespoons (30 mL)
olive oil

Zest and juice of 1 organic
lemon and 1 organic lime

1 tablespoon (15 mL)
thyme-infused honey
(p. 197)

2 tablespoons (30 mL)
chopped tarragon,
savory or mint

Shaved Parmesan cheese
(optional)

—

SHAVE zucchini into long strips using a vegetable peeler. Arrange on a serving platter and season.

WHISK oil, citrus zest, citrus juice and honey in a small bowl until emulsified. Season.

DRIZZLE zucchini with dressing. Garnish with herbs and Parmesan, if desired.

×

Serves 4

Fennel and Mango Salad

—

1 fennel bulb, thinly sliced crosswise using a mandoline

1 large mango (or 2 small), cut into thin strips

Juice of 2 limes

2 tablespoons (30 mL) olive oil

Sea salt and freshly cracked pepper

¼ to ½ cup (60 to 125 mL) chopped tarragon or basil

—

Variations

Replace the mango with 2 apples, 2 pears, 2 white peaches or 2 oranges.

—

COMBINE fennel, mango, lime juice and olive oil in a bowl. Season. Let stand for 20 minutes at room temperature.

GARNISH with fresh herbs just before serving.

×

Serves 4

White Peaches and Mozzarella

—

3 tablespoons (45 mL) olive oil

Sea salt and freshly cracked pepper

1 tablespoon (15 mL) white balsamic vinegar

2 balls fresh mozzarella cheese, cut into ¼-inch (5 mm) slices

2 white peaches or nectarines, quartered

1 cup (250 mL) chopped basil or tarragon

—

WHISK oil and vinegar in a small bowl. Season.

ARRANGE slices of mozzarella and peaches on a serving plate.

GARNISH with basil. Drizzle with vinaigrette.

×

Caprese Salad

—

—

3 or 4 heirloom tomatoes, sliced or quartered

1 ball buffalo mozzarella, sliced

A few leaves of oregano or basil

2 to 3 tablespoons (30 to 45 mL) best quality olive oil

1 tablespoon (15 mL) balsamic vinegar reduction (see p. 206)

Sea salt and freshly cracked pepper

ARRANGE tomatoes on a large serving platter or 4 individual plates. Add the mozzarella.

GARNISH with herbs. Drizzle with oil and a few drops of balsamic vinegar reduction. Season.

×

Serves 4 to 6

Tabbouleh

—

½ cup (125 mL) bulgur

2 cups (500 mL) diced fresh tomatoes (with their juices)

2 cups (500 mL) chopped parsley

1 cup (250 mL) chopped mint

4 green onions, finely chopped

Juice of 1 to 2 lemons

½ cup (125 mL) olive oil

½ teaspoon (2 mL) cinnamon + ½ teaspoon (2 mL) ground allspice

Sea salt and freshly cracked pepper

SOAK bulgur for 10 minutes in a bowl of cold water. Drain well and return to the bowl.

STIR in tomatoes and their juice.

ADD remaining ingredients. Mix well. Season.

×

Greek Salad

1 red onion, cut into
6 wedges

3 garlic cloves, minced

Juice of 1 lemon

Leaves from 3 thyme sprigs

Leaves from 6 oregano
sprigs, chopped

¼ cup (60 mL) olive oil

4 tomatoes, cut into
6 wedges

3 mini or Lebanese
cucumbers, sliced

1 sweet yellow pepper,
cut into large pieces

1 heart of romaine,
coarsely chopped

½ cup (125 mL) pitted
Kalamata olives

1 cup (250 mL) crumbled
sheep's milk feta cheese

Variation

Greek basil has smaller
leaves than Thai or Italian
basil and is very good in a
Greek salad. It is so fragrant
it is almost spicy.

PREHEAT grill to high. Grill onions until slightly charred. Reserve.

WHISK garlic, lemon juice, thyme, oregano and oil in a small bowl until emulsified and creamy. Reserve.

COMBINE tomatoes, cucumbers, pepper, lettuce and grilled red onions in a large bowl. Drizzle with dressing and toss. Sprinkle with olives and feta.

Watermelon Salad with Feta

134

—

4 cups (1 L) arugula

3 to 4 cups (750 mL to 1 L) cubed watermelon

Juice of 1 lime

¼ cup (60 mL) infused olive oil (see below)

¼ red onion, finely chopped (or 1 teaspoon/5 mL chopped chives)

4 oz (120 g) feta cheese

12 mint leaves, chopped

Sea salt and freshly cracked pepper

—

Infused Olive Oil

Gently heat 1 cup (250 mL) olive oil in a small saucepan. Add 2 sprigs of rosemary, sage or thyme. Steep for 20 minutes off the heat. Remove the branches. The oil will keep for several weeks.

—

Variations

Replace the watermelon with papaya, another type of melon or strawberries.

If using strawberries, replace the lime juice with 2 tbsp of aged balsamic vinegar or balsamic reduction (p. 206).

—

DIVIDE arugula and watermelon among individual bowls.

DRIZZLE with lime juice and a dash of oil.

GARNISH with red onion, feta and mint. Season.

×

Arugula with Pears and Grapes

—

6 cups (1.5 L) arugula

24 red grapes

2 pears, cored and
cut into thin slices

Leaves from
1 bunch cilantro

3 tablespoons (45 mL)
olive oil

1 teaspoon (5 mL)
orange oil (optional)

1 tablespoon (15 mL)
balsamic vinegar

Sea salt and freshly
cracked pepper

Coarsely chopped
hazelnuts

Shaved Pecorino
Romano cheese

—

TOSS arugula, grapes, pears and cilantro in a large bowl.

WHISK together oils and vinegar. Pour over salad and toss.

SEASON. Garnish with hazelnuts and Pecorino.

×

Fiddlehead Salad

—

3 tablespoons (45 mL) olive oil

2 young garlic cloves, chopped

2 cups (500 mL) fiddleheads, blanched for 1 minute

2 parsnips, thinly sliced

2 cups (500 mL) oyster or other mushrooms

Juice of 1 lemon

Sea salt and freshly cracked pepper

—

HEAT oil and garlic in a skillet over medium heat. Add fiddleheads and parsnips. Cook for 3 minutes, stirring often.

ADD the mushrooms and cook for 2 to 3 minutes, or until mushrooms have browned.

DRIZZLE vegetables with lemon juice and season. Serve warm or at room temperature.

×

Spinach Salad with Haloumi

—

2 tablespoons (30 mL) olive oil

½ lb (225 g) haloumi cheese, cut into ¼-inch (5 mm) slices

5 cups (1.25 L) baby spinach or watercress

½ cup (125 mL) coarsely chopped parsley

1 pomegranate, seeded

Juice of 1 lemon

—

HEAT 1 tbsp (15 mL) oil in a skillet over high heat. Cook haloumi slices for 2 minutes per side or until golden.

ARRANGE spinach on plates, drizzle with remaining 1 tbsp (15 mL) oil and top with slices of haloumi.

GARNISH with parsley, pomegranate seeds and a squeeze of lemon juice.

×

Roasted Fennel and Tomato Salad with Mozzarella

—

1 fennel bulb

Juice of 1 lemon

2 tablespoons (30 mL) olive oil

3 tablespoons (45 mL) grated Parmesan cheese

2 branches cherry tomatoes on the vine (about 1 cup/250 mL)

2 balls mozzarella, sliced

Sea salt and freshly cracked pepper

2 cups (500 mL) arugula

½ cup (125 mL) basil leaves

—

Variation

This dish works well with simply the Parmesan-crusted fennel, omitting the tomatoes and mozzarella.

—

PREHEAT oven to 400°F (200°C).

SLICE fennel lengthwise ¼ inch (5 mm) thick.

PLACE slices on a baking sheet and drizzle with half the lemon juice and olive oil. Sprinkle with Parmesan. Cover with foil and roast for 20 to 25 minutes or until tender and cheese is melted.

LAY the cherry tomatoes on a separate baking sheet. Drizzle with remaining olive oil. Roast, uncovered, for 15 minutes.

UNCOVER fennel and cook for another 5 minutes to lightly colour.

ARRANGE fennel on a large platter. Drizzle with remaining lemon juice. Garnish with the tomatoes and mozzarella slices. Season.

SERVE with arugula and basil leaves. Finish with a drizzle of olive oil, if desired.

×

Roasted Eggplant with Feta

—

—

1 eggplant

1 to 2 tablespoons
(15 to 30 mL) olive oil

Sea salt and freshly
cracked pepper

4 oz (120 g) sheep's milk
feta cheese, crumbled

1 cup (250 mL) coarsely
chopped flat-leaf parsley

½ pomegranate, seeded

Juice of ½ lemon

PREHEAT oven to 375°F (190°C).

CUT eggplant lengthwise into ½-inch (1 cm) slices.

PLACE eggplant slices on a parchment-lined baking sheet. Drizzle with oil and season. Bake for 20 minutes.

TOP eggplant slices with feta and bake for another 10 minutes or until cheese has melted.

GARNISH with parsley and pomegranate seeds, and drizzle with lemon juice.

×

Grilled Corn

—

—

6 corncobs, with husks

3 tablespoons (45 mL)
mayonnaise

3 tablespoons (45 mL)
grated Parmesan cheese

Cayenne

1 lime, cut in wedges

PREHEAT grill to high.

GRILL corncobs in their husks for 15 to 20 minutes or until corn is tender. Let cool for 15 minutes, then peel.

BRUSH ears with mayonnaise. Sprinkle with Parmesan and a pinch of cayenne.

SERVE with lime wedges.

×

Waldorf Salad

—

3 tablespoons (45 mL) currants

3 tablespoons (45 mL) boiling water

1 Granny Smith apple, unpeeled, cut into batons

1 Pink Lady apple, unpeeled, cut into batons

Juice of 1 lemon

3 celery stalks, thinly sliced on the diagonal

2 tablespoons (30 mL) chopped celery leaves

2 endives

¼ cup (60 mL) mayonnaise

2 tablespoons (30 mL) yogurt

4 oz (120 g) Roquefort cheese, cut into small pieces

3 tablespoons (45 mL) boiling water

Sea salt and freshly cracked pepper

3 tablespoons (45 mL) walnuts with tamari and maple syrup (p. 205)

—

REHYDRATE currants in 3 tbsp (45 mL) boiling water. Let sit for 10 minutes. Drain.

PLACE apples in a bowl. Add lemon juice, celery, celery leaves and endive leaves. Toss gently.

WHISK together mayonnaise, yogurt and half the Roquefort. Add 3 tbsp (45 mL) boiling water, whisking vigorously to produce a smooth, creamy dressing. Season.

DIVIDE salad among plates. Top with remaining Roquefort and drizzle with dressing. Garnish with walnuts and currants.

×

Grilled Squash Salad with Stilton

—

¼ cup (60 mL) olive oil

1 small butternut squash, peeled and thinly sliced

Sea salt and freshly cracked pepper

4 sage leaves

2 cups (500 mL) watercress or arugula

4 oz (120 g) Stilton cheese, crumbled

2 tablespoons (30 mL) walnut or hazelnut oil

Freshly grated nutmeg

—

HEAT oil in a large nonstick skillet over medium heat. Add squash slices and season with salt and pepper.

COOK for 3 to 4 minutes per side or until squash is tender and golden, adding sage halfway through.

DIVIDE greens among 4 plates. Top with slices of squash. Sprinkle with Stilton, drizzle with walnut oil and season. Sprinkle with a pinch of nutmeg.

×

Roasted Winter Vegetables

—

4 parsnips, sliced lengthwise

4 carrots, sliced lengthwise

4 beets, peeled and quartered

1 red onion, quartered

¼ cup (60 mL) olive oil

4 garlic cloves, crushed with the flat of a knife

Sea salt and freshly cracked pepper

Juice of 1 lemon

½ cup (125 mL) chopped flat-leaf parsley

Shaved Parmesan cheese

—

PREHEAT oven to 400°F (200°C).

COMBINE all vegetables in a large bowl. Add olive oil and garlic. Season. Mix well.

SPREAD on a baking sheet and cover with foil. Roast for 20 to 25 minutes or until vegetables are just tender.

UNCOVER and roast for another 10 minutes. Transfer to a serving bowl.

DRIZZLE with lemon juice, sprinkle with parsley and garnish with Parmesan.

×

Plantain Salad

—

1 cup (250 mL) olive oil

1 plantain, cut into ½-inch (1 cm) rounds

1 green apple, unpeeled, thinly sliced

1 celery stalk, thinly sliced on the diagonal

1 cup (250 mL) chopped cilantro

2 cups (500 mL) watercress

1 medium red chili pepper, finely chopped

Juice of 1 to 2 limes

Sea salt and freshly cracked pepper

—

HEAT oil in a skillet over medium heat. Add plantain rounds and fry for 2 to 3 minutes per side, or until golden. Drain on paper towels.

MIX all other ingredients in a serving bowl. Add the warm plantains. Season and serve.

×

Fava Bean and Sweet Potato Salad

—

4 cups (1 L) sweet potato, cut into ¾-inch (2 cm) cubes

2 tablespoons (30 mL) olive oil

1 medium red onion, finely chopped

2 garlic cloves, chopped

1 bird's eye chili, slit lengthwise

2 teaspoons (10 mL) grated fresh ginger

2 teaspoons (10 mL) mustard seeds + 2 teaspoons (10 mL) cumin seeds

1 cup (250 mL) peeled blanched shelled fava beans

Sea salt and freshly cracked pepper

2 cups (500 mL) greens (such as baby spinach, dandelion, watercress)

1 cup (250 mL) coarsely chopped cilantro

Juice of 1 lime

—

Variation

Replace the fava beans with blanched shelled edamame (p. 91).

COOK sweet potato in a large pot of boiling salted water for 7 minutes or until just tender. Drain.

HEAT oil in a large skillet over medium heat. Cook onion, garlic, chili, ginger, mustard seeds and cumin seeds for 5 minutes or until onion is softened.

ADD sweet potato and cook for 7 minutes or until golden, stirring gently and often without crushing potatoes. Remove chili.

STIR in fava beans and cook for a few minutes to warm through. Adjust seasoning.

PLACE greens and cilantro in serving dishes. Top with sweet potato mixture and finish with a squeeze of lime.

×

Cuban Salad

—

5 cups (1.25 L) water

1 cup (250 mL) dried red or
black beans, soaked overnight

2 or 3 thyme sprigs

1 tablespoon (15 mL)
coriander seeds

2 cups (500 mL)
cherry tomatoes, quartered

¼ cup (60 mL) olive oil

Sea salt and freshly
cracked pepper

1 to 2 firm mangoes, cubed

1 avocado, cubed

Juice of 2 limes

½ red onion, chopped

1 green onion, chopped

½ chili pepper, finely chopped

1 cup (250 mL) corn kernels
(frozen or fresh, see below)

1 to 2 cups (250 to 500 mL)
coarsely chopped cilantro

—

Corn

In season, fresh corn is always
preferable over frozen. Remove
the raw kernels simply by cutting
along the hard cob. This way, you
won't have to cook the ears in a
large quantity of water.

—

BOIL water in a large saucepan. Add
beans, thyme and coriander seeds.
Cook for about 1 hour, until beans
are just tender. Drain without rinsing,
and refrigerate for 30 minutes.

PLACE tomatoes in a large bowl.
Add oil, salt and pepper. Let stand
for 10 minutes.

ADD beans and remaining
ingredients. Toss to combine and
adjust seasoning.

×

Melon Salad with Orange Blossom Water

—

1 tablespoon (15 mL)
white balsamic vinegar

1 tablespoon (15 mL)
maple syrup

2 tablespoons (30 mL)
orange blossom water

3 tablespoons (45 mL)
olive oil

½ cantaloupe or other
melon (or 6 peaches), sliced

½ cup (125 mL) watercress

½ cup (125 mL) coarsely
chopped young chard

12 slices bresaola
or prosciutto

Toasted sliced almonds

Sea salt and freshly
cracked pepper

—

WHISK vinegar, maple syrup, orange blossom water and oil in a small bowl until dressing is thick and creamy.

ARRANGE melon slices on plates. Top with greens and drizzle with dressing.

GARNISH salad with bresaola and almonds. Season and serve.

×

Wild Rice Salad with Green Beans and Herbs

—

1 cup (250 mL) wild rice

1 cup (250 mL) green beans or runner beans

3 tablespoons (45 mL) pine nuts

1 small red onion, finely chopped

1 sweet red pepper, diced

½ cup (125 mL) chopped mint

½ cup (125 mL) chopped dill, basil, cilantro or flat-leaf parsley

Zest and juice of 1 organic lemon

2 to 3 tablespoons (30 to 45 mL) olive oil

Sea salt and freshly cracked pepper

—

COOK wild rice according to package instructions. Drain and let cool.

BLANCH beans for 3 to 4 minutes in boiling salted water. Cool quickly under cold running water to retain colour. Slice thickly on the diagonal.

TOAST pine nuts in a dry skillet for a few minutes over medium-high heat until golden.

PLACE rice in a large bowl. Stir in beans, pine nuts and remaining ingredients. Season and mix well.

×

Italian-Style Lentil Salad

—

3 cups (750 mL) water

1 cup (250 mL) green lentils
or lentils du Puy

2 garlic cloves
(1 whole and 1 minced)

1 cup (250 mL) tomato confit
(see below)

1 roasted sweet red pepper,
cut into strips

1 chili pepper, finely chopped

Zest and juice of 1 organic lemon

3 tablespoons olive oil

1 cup (250 mL) coarsely chopped
basil or flat-leaf parsley

½ cup (125 mL) shaved Grana
Padano or Parmesan cheese

Sea salt and freshly cracked
pepper

—

Tomato Confit

Place 8 Roma tomatoes, quartered,
or 1 cup (250 mL) cherry tomatoes
on a parchment-lined baking
sheet. Add a few thyme sprigs,
season and sprinkle, with a bit of
cane sugar if desired. Drizzle with
olive oil. Bake at 375°F (190°C) for
15 to 20 minutes or until tender
and sweet.

—

Variation

You can replace the tomatoes with
⅓ cup (80 mL) sun-dried tomatoes
or 1 cup (250 mL) sliced fresh
tomatoes with olive oil.

—

BOIL salted water in a saucepan. Add lentils and whole garlic clove. Reduce heat and simmer for 20 minutes or until lentils are just tender. Drain without rinsing.

TRANSFER lentils to a bowl. Add remaining ingredients, including minced garlic. Season and mix well.

×

Lentil Salad with Feta and Grapes

—

3 cups (750 mL) water

1 cup (250 mL) green lentils
or lentils du Puy

2 garlic cloves
(1 whole and 1 minced)

1½ cups (375 mL)
green grapes, quartered

1 cup (250 mL) Greek feta,
broken into chunks

1 cup (250 mL) coarsely
chopped cilantro

3 tablespoons (45 mL)
olive oil

1 chili pepper, finely
chopped

Zest and juice of
1 organic lemon

—

Marinade for Steak

Combine 1 grated small
onion, 1 tablespoon (15 mL)
sherry vinegar, 1 tablespoon
(15 mL) sumac, 1 tablespoon
(15 mL) ground coriander
and a pinch of ground
allspice. Marinate flank or
skirt steak for 2 hours in
refrigerator.

—

BOIL salted water in a saucepan. Add lentils and whole garlic clove. Reduce heat and simmer for 20 minutes or until lentils are just tender.

DRAIN without rinsing. Let cool.

COMBINE all other ingredients, including minced garlic, in a bowl. Gently stir in lentils.

SERVE lentil salad warm or at room temperature, topped with slices of grilled marinated steak, if desired (see below).

×

Quinoa Salad with Beets

—

2 cups (500 mL) water

1 medium beet,
peeled and diced

1 cup (250 mL) red quinoa,
rinsed thoroughly

1 Granny Smith apple,
unpeeled, cut into
matchsticks

¼ cup (60 mL) coarsely
chopped hazelnuts

½ cup (125 mL) chopped
flat-leaf parsley

1 tablespoon (15 mL)
chopped mint

1 tablespoon (15 mL)
chopped cilantro

2 tablespoons (30 mL)
olive oil

1 tablespoon (15 mL)
cider vinegar

Sea salt and freshly
cracked pepper

—

Variation

Hazelnuts can be replaced
with pistachios for a nice
contrast of colours.

—

BOIL water in a large pot. Cook beets over medium heat for 15 minutes or until just tender. Remove beets, reserving cooking water.

ADD quinoa to the pot of cooking water. Simmer over low heat for 15 minutes or until quinoa is cooked. Drain.

COMBINE all ingredients in a bowl. Season, stir and serve.

×

Lamb Salad with Tomato and Feta

—

1¾ lb (800 g) lamb sirloin

Sea salt and freshly cracked pepper

4 tablespoons (60 mL) olive oil

3 tablespoons (45 mL) honey

2 tablespoons (30 mL) cider vinegar

4 green onions, chopped

6 Roma tomatoes, cut into 6 wedges

8 Medjool dates, cut into 6 wedges

½ cup (125 mL) flat-leaf parsley

½ cup (125 mL) cilantro

½ cup (125 mL) arugula

5 oz (150 g) feta cheese, cut into pieces

15 pitted black olives

—

PREHEAT oven to 400°F (200°C).

TRIM fat from lamb and season meat.

HEAT 1 tbsp (15 mL) oil in an ovenproof skillet over high heat. Brown the meat for 2 minutes on each side, then transfer skillet to the oven for 4 to 10 minutes (4 minutes for rare, 10 minutes for well done). Transfer to a plate and keep warm in the oven (turned off).

POUR honey into the hot skillet and place over medium heat. When honey begins to bubble, add vinegar and remaining 3 tbsp (45 mL) oil.

ADD green onions, tomatoes and dates. Heat through for 1 minute.

DIVIDE the greens among plates. Top with tomato mixture. Slice lamb and arrange on top of salad. Top with feta and black olives.

×

Soba Noodle Salad with Bok Choy and Tofu

—

3 tablespoons (45 mL) sesame oil

1 inch (2.5 cm) fresh ginger, grated

3 garlic cloves, chopped

1 hot chili pepper, finely chopped

1 teaspoon (5 mL) curry powder

½ cup (125 mL) organic firm tofu, cubed or cut in sticks

1 medium onion, finely chopped

1 carrot, cut into matchsticks

5 shiitake mushrooms, sliced

2 bok choy, quartered

1 cup (250 mL) chopped mint

Juice of 1 lime

1 lb (500 g) soba noodles, cooked and rinsed in cold water

Sea salt and freshly cracked pepper

2 tablespoons (30 mL) peanuts or sesame seeds

—

Variation

Instead of mixing tofu and sesame seeds into the salad, prepare tofu schnitzel (p. 217) separately, as in the photo.

—

HEAT oil in a wok over high heat. Sauté ginger, garlic, chili, curry and tofu for 1 minute, stirring constantly.

ADD onion. Cook, stirring often, for 2 minutes.

MIX in carrot and 1 tbsp (15 mL) water. Cook for 3 minutes or until carrot is tender.

ADD shiitakes and bok choy; cook for 2 minutes.

STIR in mint and lime juice. Remove from heat. Add noodles and toss gently. Season.

SERVE salad warm or at room temperature, garnished with peanuts or sesame seeds.

×

Serves 4

Salade Niçoise

—

2 cups (500 mL)
green beans

2 cups (500 mL)
halved new potatoes

1½ teaspoons (7 mL)
Dijon mustard

1½ teaspoons (7 mL)
red wine vinegar

Juice of ½ lemon

¼ cup (60 mL) olive oil

¼ to ½ red onion,
thinly sliced

Sea salt and freshly
cracked pepper

8 to 10 marinated
white anchovies

—

Marinated
white anchovies

These delicious
anchovies can be found
in Mediterranean grocery
stores. You can replace
them with sardines or
a few spoonfuls of cod
chiquetaille (p. 173).

—

BLANCH beans for 3 to 4 minutes in boiling salted water. Remove with tongs or a slotted spoon and cool quickly by running under cold water to preserve their colour. Reserve.

PLACE potatoes in the same boiling water and cook for 5 minutes or until just tender. Drain without rinsing.

COMBINE mustard, vinegar and lemon juice in a large bowl. Add oil in a thin stream while whisking until emulsified.

ADD potatoes while still warm and toss to coat with dressing. Stir in onion and beans. Season.

SERVE salad warm or at room temperature, garnished with marinated white anchovies.

×

Green Bean and New Potato Salad

—

3 tablespoons (45 mL) olive oil

1 teaspoon (5 mL) smoked paprika

1 celery stalk, finely diced

2 cups (500 mL) beans (yellow, green or both)

2 cups (500 mL) halved new potatoes

Juice of 1 lemon

1 tablespoon (15 mL) chopped celery leaves

3 green onions, sliced on the diagonal

1 cup (250 mL) mâche or other greens

Sea salt and freshly cracked pepper

—

COMBINE oil, paprika and celery in a large bowl. Reserve.

BLANCH beans in boiling salted water for 3 to 4 minutes. Remove with tongs or a slotted spoon and cool quickly under cold running water to preserve their colour. Reserve.

COOK potatoes in the same boiling water for 5 minutes or until just tender. Drain without rinsing.

TRANSFER hot potatoes to the bowl of celery mixture, add lemon juice and stir gently to avoid crushing potatoes.

ADD reserved beans, celery leaves, green onions and greens. Season.

×

Fig Salad with Chorizo

—

1 tablespoon (15 mL) olive oil

1 chorizo, sliced into ½-inch (1 cm) rounds

2 young garlic cloves, crushed

8 dried Turkish figs

½ cup (125 mL) sherry vinegar

½ cup (125 mL) white balsamic vinegar

1 cup (250 mL) cane sugar

1 cup (250 mL) water

1 cinnamon stick

2 whole cloves

3 cups (750 mL) watercress

—

HEAT oil in a skillet over medium-high heat. Fry chorizo and garlic for 3 minutes or until sausage is browned. Remove from heat.

PLACE figs in a small saucepan with vinegars, sugar, water, cinnamon and cloves. Simmer over low heat for 10 minutes to rehydrate figs.

DIVIDE watercress among plates. Top with chorizo and figs. Drizzle with fig cooking liquid.

×

Cherry Tomato and Blueberry Salad with Chorizo

—

3 cups (750 mL) cherry tomatoes, halved

¼ cup (60 mL) + 1 tablespoon (15 mL) olive oil

Sea salt and freshly cracked pepper

1 chorizo, sliced into ½-inch (1 cm) rounds

2 young garlic cloves, crushed

1 cup (250 mL) blueberries

1 cup (250 mL) coarsely chopped flat-leaf parsley

½ cup (125 mL) coarsely chopped mint

2 tablespoons (30 mL) white balsamic vinegar (or juice of ½ lemon)

—

Variation

This salad is delicious without chorizo, either alone or with feta or mozzarella.

—

PLACE tomatoes in a large bowl. Add ¼ cup (60 mL) oil, salt and pepper. Marinate for 10 minutes.

HEAT remaining 1 tbsp (15 mL) oil in a skillet over medium-high heat. Fry chorizo and garlic for 3 minutes or until sausage is browned. Remove from heat.

ADD blueberries to tomatoes, stirring gently to avoid crushing. Stir in parsley, mint and vinegar. Season.

SERVE salad topped with slices of chorizo.

×

Plum and Sesame Chicken Salad

—

3 tablespoons (45 mL) olive oil

1 tablespoon (15 mL) white balsamic vinegar

Juice of 1 lemon

4 firm, ripe purple plums, cut into 6 wedges

3 cups (750 mL) baby spinach or mâche

⅔ cup (160 mL) coarsely chopped mint

Sea salt and freshly cracked pepper

1 recipe chicken schnitzel (see below)

—

Chicken Schnitzel

Place a boneless, skinless chicken breast, cut into strips, in marinade for tofu schnitzel (p. 217). Dredge chicken pieces in flour, then in egg and then in sesame seeds before frying.

POUR oil, vinegar and lemon juice into a small bowl. Whisk until emulsified.

PLACE plums, spinach and mint in a bowl. Season, drizzle with dressing and toss.

ARRANGE on plates and top with chicken schnitzel.

×

Cod Chiquetaille

173

—

1 lb (500 g) salt cod

1 cup (250 mL) white balsamic vinegar

½ cup (125 mL) olive oil

1 cup (250 mL) shredded green cabbage

½ cup (125 mL) grated carrot

4 shallots, minced

2 garlic cloves, minced

1 Scotch bonnet pepper or other small hot pepper, minced (wear rubber gloves)

—

Variation

This is also a delicious tapas spread on toast. Well covered with the balsamic vinegar, it keeps for 1 month or more in the refrigerator.

—

SOAK cod overnight in 12 cups (3 L) water. Drain, change water and boil fish for 10 minutes. Drain, change water and boil for another 10 minutes. Drain and refrigerate.

MIX all other ingredients in a bowl and let stand for 2 hours at room temperature.

SHRED cooled cod with two forks and stir into cabbage mixture.

USE cod chiquetaille to enhance the flavour of an avocado, a salad, rice, etc.

×

Pappardelle Salad with Tomatoes and Asparagus

16 medium
asparagus spears

1½ cups (375 mL)
quartered tomatoes

3 tablespoons (45 mL)
olive oil

Sea salt and freshly
cracked pepper

Zest and juice of
1 organic lemon

Leaves from 8 oregano
sprigs, chopped

1 lb (500 g) egg pappardelle

BLANCH asparagus for 3 minutes in a pot of boiling salted water.

DRAIN and cool quickly by running under cold water so they retain their colour. Cut into thirds and reserve.

COMBINE tomatoes with 1 tbsp (15 mL) oil in a small bowl. Season with salt and pepper.

PLACE lemon juice and zest in a large serving bowl. Add oregano and remaining 2 tbsp (30 mL) oil. Stir and season.

COOK pasta until al dente. Drain without rinsing. Transfer to the serving bowl and mix well.

GARNISH with tomatoes and asparagus. Serve salad warm or at room temperature.

×

Orecchiette Salad with Duck and Rapini

—

1 lb (500 g) orecchiette or other short pasta

2 to 3 tablespoons (30 to 45 mL) olive oil

1 leek, white part only, thinly sliced

1 cup (250 mL) blanched rapini, cut into 1-inch (2.5 cm) pieces

2 confit duck legs, shredded

2 tablespoons (30 mL) lime juice

Sea salt and freshly cracked pepper

Red pepper flakes (optional)

—

COOK pasta until al dente. Drain, reserving about ½ cup (125 mL) cooking water.

HEAT 1 tbsp (15 mL) oil in a large skillet over low heat. Cook leek with 1 tbsp (15 mL) water for 3 minutes to soften.

ADD blanched rapini and duck. Cook for 3 minutes, stirring, until mixture is hot.

STIR in drained pasta.

DRIZZLE with lime juice. Add oil or pasta water as needed. Season, and add red pepper flakes to taste, if desired. Serve warm.

×

Farfalle Salad with Lobster

—

2 tablespoons (30 mL)
olive oil

2 leeks, thinly sliced

Juice of 2 limes

12 asparagus spears,
cut into thirds

2 cups (500 mL)
cherry tomatoes, halved

½ cup (125 mL) tarragon
leaves + 4 tarragon sprigs

½ cup (125 mL) pastis

1 lb (500 g) farfalle or
other short pasta

2 cooked lobsters
(or 4 to 6 crab claws),
shelled

2 tablespoons (30 mL)
butter, melted

—

HEAT oil in a large skillet over low heat. Cook leeks with 1 tbsp (15 mL) water for 3 minutes, until softened.

POUR in ⅓ cup (80 mL) water and lime juice. Add asparagus and cook for 2 minutes.

ADD tomatoes and tarragon leaves. Continue cooking for another 2 minutes, then add pastis. Remove from heat.

COOK pasta until al dente. Drain, reserving a little cooking water.

STIR pasta into skillet. Add about 3 tbsp (45 mL) cooking water to form a sauce.

MIX lobster meat and melted butter in a small bowl.

DIVIDE pasta among warm serving plates and top with lobster. Garnish with a sprig of tarragon and serve.

×

Pita Chips

—

2 tablespoons (30 mL) olive oil

1 tablespoon (15 mL) sumac or ground cumin

4 pitas, cut into triangles

—

PREHEAT oven to 375°F (190°C).

MIX olive oil with sumac. Brush on pitas.

BAKE for 7 to 8 minutes or until pitas are golden.

×

Muhammara— Red Pepper Purée with Walnuts

—

1 cup (250 mL) walnuts or pecans

1 teaspoon (5 mL) cumin seeds

3 roasted sweet red peppers

2 tablespoons (30 mL) olive oil

1 tablespoon (15 mL) pomegranate molasses (see below)

1 tablespoon (15 mL) water

A pinch of cayenne (or ½ chili pepper, seeded)

½ slice toast, crust removed

Sea salt

—

Pomegranate molasses

Both sweet and sour, this molasses can replace a balsamic vinegar reduction (p. 206) on grilled fish or a dessert. It can be found in Middle Eastern grocery stores.

—

TOAST nuts and cumin in a dry skillet over medium-low heat until nuts are golden and fragrant.

GRIND nut mixture with remaining ingredients, except toast, in a food processor, gradually adding toast to thicken until a spreadable consistency is achieved. Salt to taste.

×

Baba Ganoush Tartine with Mozzarella

—

2 balls mozzarella, sliced

2 ciabatta buns, halved

½ cup (125 mL) baba ganoush (see next page)

1 tablespoon (15 mL) gremolata (p. 55)

8 basil leaves

—

PAT mozzarella slices with a paper towel to remove any excess moisture.

PLACE mozzarella on bread and top with baba ganoush, a little gremolata and a few basil leaves.

×

Baba Ganoush

189

—

1 eggplant, peeled and thickly sliced

2 tablespoons (30 mL) olive oil

Sea salt and freshly cracked pepper

Juice of 1 lemon

1 tablespoon (15 mL) 10% yogurt (optional)

—

Variations

Have fun flavouring baba ganoush:

Syrian: add 1 tablespoon (15 mL) pomegranate molasses (see p. 186)

Greek: add 1 tablespoon (15 mL) crumbled feta

Lebanese: add 1 tablespoon (15 mL) tahini

—

BRUSH eggplant slices with oil and season with salt and pepper. Cook over medium heat on a barbecue or in a skillet for 4 to 5 minutes per side or until browned. Let cool.

MASH with a fork or in a food processor to achieve desired consistency. Season to taste. Add a little lemon juice and yogurt, if desired.

SERVE with pita chips (p. 186) or spread on a sandwich.

×

Marinated Red Onion

Thinly slice a red onion and place in a small bowl. Stir in ¼ cup (60 mL) white balsamic or sherry vinegar. Marinate for 1 hour at room temperature. Can be refrigerated in an airtight container and kept for up to 2 weeks.

Serves 4

Hummus

—

2 cups (500 mL)
cooked chickpeas

½ cup (125 mL) olive oil

Zest and juice of
1 organic lemon

2 garlic cloves

1 tablespoon (15 mL) tahini

1 teaspoon (5 mL)
ground cumin

Sea salt and freshly
ground pepper

—

PURÉE all ingredients in a food processor.
Season.

SERVE with pita chips (p. 186) or spread on
a sandwich.

×

Serves 4

Hummus Tartine with Dates

—

1½ cups (375 mL)
hummus (see above)

4 slices bread, toasted

1 roasted sweet red pepper,
cut into strips

⅓ cup (80 mL) marinated
red onion (see opposite)

6 Medjool dates, quartered

1 cup (250 mL)
baby spinach, watercress
or arugula

Zest of 1 organic lemon
(optional)

—

SPREAD 3 tablespoons (45 mL) of hummus
on each slice of bread.

GARNISH with red pepper, marinated
red onion, dates, greens and lemon zest,
if desired.

×

Roasted Vegetable Sandwich with Goat Cheese

½ eggplant,
sliced lengthwise

Sea salt and freshly
cracked pepper

2 tablespoons (30 mL)
olive oil

½ sweet red pepper

1 zucchini,
sliced lengthwise

1 baguette,
cut in half lengthwise

2 tablespoons (30 mL)
mayonnaise mixed with
1 teaspoon (5 mL) pesto

2 oz (60 g) fresh goat cheese
(or 2 balls mozzarella),
sliced

6 chives

6 to 8 basil leaves or leaves
from 2 to 3 oregano sprigs

PREHEAT oven to 375°F (190°C).

PLACE eggplant slices on a parchment-lined baking sheet. Season and drizzle with 1 tbsp (15 mL) oil. Add red pepper, cut side down.

ROAST for 25 minutes or until eggplant and pepper are browned. Cool. Peel pepper and cut into strips.

PLACE zucchini on a separate parchment-lined baking sheet. Season and drizzle with remaining 1 tbsp (15 mL) oil. Roast for 10 minutes.

SPREAD one side of baguette with pesto mayonnaise. Arrange eggplant, pepper, zucchini and goat cheese on top. Season and garnish with fresh herbs.

COVER with baguette top and slice according to the number of servings desired.

×

Goat Cheese Tartine with Apricot Purée

—

1 cup (250 mL)
dried apricots

⅓ cup (80 mL) boiling water

1 teaspoon (5 mL)
white balsamic vinegar

4 slices whole-grain
bread, toasted

1 cup (250 mL)
fresh goat cheese

8 chives

½ cup (125 mL)
chiffonade of basil

1½ cups (375 mL)
arugula

—

Variation

Replace the apricots with
dried pears. Replace the
white balsamic vinegar with
another light vinegar (pear
or champagne).

—

COVER dried apricots with boiling water and let sit for 10 minutes or until softened.

PURÉE in a blender. Add vinegar.

SPREAD toast with goat cheese. Garnish with apricot purée, chives, basil and arugula.

×

Brie Tartine with White Peaches

—

1 white peach or nectarine, sliced

1 teaspoon (5 mL) white balsamic vinegar

Sea salt and freshly cracked pepper

4 slices Brie, at room temperature

2 slices bread

3 tablespoons (45 mL) coarsely chopped hazelnuts

8 basil or mint leaves, chopped

—

PLACE peach slices in a small bowl. Drizzle with vinegar and toss gently. Season with salt and pepper.

PLACE 2 slices of Brie on each slice of bread. Top with peach slices and garnish with nuts and basil.

×

Brie Tartine with Asparagus

—

6 asparagus spears

2 slices bread

4 slices Brie, at room temperature

1 tablespoon (15 mL) thyme-infused honey (see opposite)

3 tablespoons (45 mL) coarsely chopped pecans with tamari and maple syrup (p. 205)

8 basil leaves

—

BLANCH asparagus for 3 minutes, then run under cold water. Pat dry.

TOP each piece of bread with 2 slices of Brie and 3 asparagus spears.

DRIZZLE with honey. Garnish with pecans and basil.

×

Thyme-Infused Honey

Gently heat 3 tbsp (45 mL) honey with 2 thyme sprigs in a small saucepan for about 5 minutes without boiling. Remove from heat and let sit before using in a sandwich.

Warm Camembert and Mushrooms Tartine

—

A small or medium wheel of Camembert cheese

1 tablespoon (15 mL) butter or olive oil

2 cups (500 mL) chopped mixed mushrooms

1 garlic clove, chopped

Sea salt and freshly cracked pepper

¼ cup (60 mL) dry white wine (optional)

¾ cup (180 mL) walnuts or pecans with tamari and honey (p. 205)

¼ cup (60 mL) chopped parsley

1 tablespoon (15 mL) truffle oil (optional)

1 small loaf bread, sliced

—

PREHEAT oven to 350°F (180°C).

PLACE wheel of cheese on a baking sheet and bake for 20 minutes or until centre is melted. Remove from oven. Pierce the centre of the wheel with the tip of a knife so that the cheese oozes out.

HEAT butter in a large skillet over medium-high heat. Add mushrooms and sauté for 2 to 3 minutes, until lightly browned.

ADD garlic and season. Continue cooking for 1 minute, then deglaze with wine, if desired. Cook for 2 more minutes. Remove from heat.

STIR in nuts and parsley. Top Camembert wheel with mushroom mixture. Drizzle with truffle oil, if desired, and serve with bread.

×

Portobello and Spinach Tartine

—

4 portobello mushrooms,
stems removed

4 garlic cloves, sliced

3 tablespoons (45 mL)
olive oil

Juice of 1 lemon

1 tablespoon (15 mL)
thyme leaves

2 cups (500 mL)
baby spinach

5 oz (150 g) Taleggio cheese,
sliced

4 slices bread, toasted

Aged balsamic vinegar or
balsamic reduction (p. 206)

—

PREHEAT oven to 400°F (200°C).

PLACE mushrooms on a parchment-lined baking sheet, stem side up. Top with garlic slices.

WHISK together oil, half the lemon juice and thyme in a small bowl. Pour over mushrooms. Bake for 10 minutes or until softened and browned.

TOP mushrooms with spinach and sliced Taleggio cheese and bake for another 6 minutes or until cheese is melted.

DIVIDE mushrooms among toast slices. Drizzle with remaining lemon juice and a dash of balsamic vinegar.

×

Fontina and Mushroom Grilled Cheese Sandwich

—

2 tablespoons (30 mL) butter

1 tablespoon (15 mL) olive oil

1½ cups (375 mL) sliced chanterelle, oyster or portobello mushrooms

1 garlic clove, chopped

1 teaspoon (5 mL) chopped rosemary

4 slices bread

2 slices Fontina or Taleggio cheese

1 teaspoon (5 mL) truffle oil (optional)

—

HEAT butter and oil in a large skillet over high heat. Cook mushrooms for a few minutes, until golden.

REDUCE heat to medium. Add garlic and rosemary. Cook for 5 minutes.

SPREAD mushrooms on 2 slices of bread. Add cheese and top with remaining bread slices.

GRILL sandwiches in a pan over medium heat or in a sandwich press for 3 to 4 minutes per side or until cheese is melted and bread is golden brown.

OPEN sandwiches carefully and pour a few drops of truffle oil inside, if desired. Close sandwiches and serve.

×

Gouda and Red Cabbage Grilled Cheese Sandwich

—

1 cup (250 mL) shredded red cabbage

¼ cup (60 mL) cider vinegar

1 tablespoon (15 mL) cane sugar

1 teaspoon (5 mL) ground cumin

Sea salt and freshly cracked pepper

9 slices Gouda cheese

6 slices bread

—

PLACE cabbage in a bowl. Stir in vinegar, sugar and cumin. Season. Marinate for 1 hour at room temperature to wilt cabbage.

PLACE 3 slices of Gouda between 2 slices of bread.

GRILL sandwiches in a pan over medium heat or in a sandwich press for 3 to 4 minutes per side or until cheese is melted and bread is golden brown.

SEPARATE bread slices gently and add about ⅓ cup (80 mL) cabbage slaw to each sandwich. Close sandwiches and serve.

×

Pear and Roquefort Pizza

—

2 tablespoons (30 mL) olive oil

1 leek, finely chopped

1 tablespoon (15 mL) water

2 pitas (about 6 inches/ 15 cm in diameter)

3 oz (90 g) Roquefort cheese, crumbled

1 pear, cored and thinly sliced, tossed with 1 teaspoon (5 mL) lemon juice

¼ cup (60 mL) arugula

3 tablespoons (45 mL) chopped pecans with tamari and maple syrup (see below)

Sea salt and freshly cracked pepper

—

Pecans with Tamari and Maple Syrup

Toast ½ cup (125 mL) pecans or walnuts in a skillet over medium heat. Add 1 to 2 tbsp (15 to 30 mL) maple syrup or honey, stirring until evenly coated. Stir in 1 tsp (5 mL) tamari, then immediately remove from heat.

—

PREHEAT oven to 400°F (200°C).

HEAT 1 tbsp (15 mL) oil in a skillet over medium heat. Add leek and water. Cook for 10 minutes. Remove from heat.

OIL pitas lightly with remaining 1 tbsp (15 mL) oil. Top with leek and half the Roquefort. Arrange pear slices on top. Top with remaining cheese.

BAKE for 4 minutes or until cheese is melted.

GARNISH pizzas with arugula and pecans. Season and serve.

×

Fig and Prosciutto Pizza

206

—

1 pita, other thin bread or pre-baked pizza crust (6 inches/15 cm in diameter)

2 tablespoons (30 mL) olive oil

2 tablespoons (30 mL) crumbled fresh goat cheese

5 thin slices prosciutto

1 cup (250 mL) fresh figs, quartered

A few leaves of arugula and basil

Sea salt and freshly cracked pepper

1 tablespoon balsamic vinegar reduction (see below)

—

Balsamic Vinegar Reduction

Combine ½ cup (125 mL) balsamic vinegar and 3 tbsp (45 mL) cane sugar in a small saucepan. Simmer over medium heat for 10 minutes, until liquid coats the back of a spoon. Let it thicken in the refrigerator for 1 hour.

—

PREHEAT oven to 400°F (200°C).

OIL pita lightly and sprinkle with goat cheese. Top with prosciutto. Bake for 3 to 4 minutes or until cheese is melted.

TOP with figs, arugula and basil. Season.

DRIZZLE with remaining oil and balsamic vinegar reduction. Serve immediately.

×

Tomato and Mozzarella Pizza

—

1 pita or pre-baked pizza crust (6 inches/15 cm in diameter)

1 tablespoon (15 mL) olive oil

1 ball buffalo mozzarella, sliced

1 cup (250 mL) cherry tomatoes, halved

½ cup (125 mL) coarsely chopped basil

½ cup (125 mL) arugula

Sea salt and freshly cracked pepper

—

PREHEAT oven to 400°F (200°C).

OIL pita lightly and toast in oven for 3 to 4 minutes.

BLOT mozzarella slices on paper towel to remove excess moisture. Remove pita from oven and immediately top with mozzarella.

ARRANGE tomatoes on top of mozzarella. Garnish with basil and arugula.

SEASON and serve immediately with a dash of olive oil, if desired.

×

Fennel and Cherry Tomato Frittata Sandwich

—

10 eggs

¼ cup (60 mL) milk

3 tablespoons (45 mL) olive oil

1 leek, finely chopped

1 fennel bulb, thinly sliced

Leaves from 10 oregano sprigs, chopped

3 cups (750 mL) spinach

2 cups (500 mL) cherry tomatoes, halved

Sea salt and freshly cracked pepper

1 cup (250 mL) arugula

12 slices toast

—

PREHEAT oven to 400°F (200°C). Line the bottom of an 8-inch (2 L) square baking dish with a sheet of parchment paper.

WHISK eggs and milk in a bowl.

HEAT oil in a large skillet over low heat. Gently cook leek and fennel for 10 minutes. Add oregano, then remove from heat.

POUR eggs into baking dish. Submerge fennel mixture and spinach in eggs so they do not dry out in the oven. Top with tomatoes. Season.

COVER with foil and bake for 20 minutes. Remove foil and cook for another 5 minutes or until golden.

SERVE frittata warm with some arugula, between 2 slices of toast.

×

Open-Faced Egg Sandwich with Avocado and Goat Cheese

—

1 avocado

Juice of ½ lemon

½ cup (125 mL) fresh goat cheese

2 slices country-style bread

6 slices cooked bacon

1 beefsteak tomato or 2 vine tomatoes, sliced

Sea salt and freshly cracked pepper

2 eggs

4 dandelion leaves or other greens, chopped if needed

—

Beefsteak tomato

This tomato variety is distinguished by its size, of course, but also because it offers more flesh than water. It is huge and delicious!

—

MASH avocado with a fork. Stir in lemon juice and goat cheese. Spread on bread slices.

TOP with bacon and tomato slices. Season.

BOIL eggs for 3 to 4 minutes, then rinse under cold water to cool.

PEEL eggs, cut in half and place on toast. Garnish with greens.

×

Californian Quesadilla

—

1 tablespoon (15 mL)
olive oil

1 shallot, minced

1 garlic clove, chopped

A pinch of smoked paprika

3 tomatoes, chopped

Sea salt and freshly
cracked pepper

4 eggs

4 tortillas

1 avocado, sliced

10 thin asparagus spears
(or 8 green beans), blanched

2 tablespoons (30 mL)
sour cream

2 green onions, chopped

—

PREHEAT oven to 400°F (200°C).

HEAT oil in a large skillet over medium heat and cook shallots, garlic and paprika for 1 minute.

ADD tomatoes and season with salt and pepper. Cook for 5 minutes, until tomatoes begin to stew.

CRACK eggs into the skillet, making sure they don't touch. Transfer pan to the oven and bake for 10 minutes.

TOP each tortilla with 1 egg, tomato sauce, some sliced avocado, 2 or 3 asparagus spears and a little sour cream. Garnish with green onion.

×

Cheddar Scones

—

2 eggs

1 cup (250 mL) milk

Juice of 1 lemon

4 cups (1 L) unbleached all-purpose flour

1 teaspoon (5 mL) baking powder

1 teaspoon (5 mL) baking soda

1¼ cups (310 mL) cold butter, cut into pieces

1½ cups (375 mL) grated sharp Cheddar cheese

1 tablespoon (15 mL) caraway seeds, cumin seeds or chopped rosemary

Maldon salt or sea salt

—

Freezing scones

Simply place the tray of unbaked scones in the freezer for 2 hours, then transfer scones to a freezer bag. You can bake the scones directly from the freezer whenever you want one!

—

BEAT eggs and milk in a small bowl. Add lemon juice and let stand for 4 minutes.

MIX flour, baking powder, baking soda and butter in a food processor until mixture resembles bread crumbs.

ADD egg mixture and pulse until dough is just combined. Transfer dough to a large bowl.

MIX in cheese and chosen spice.

FORM dough into 12 patties. Sprinkle with a few crystals of salt. Place on a parchment-lined baking sheet.

REFRIGERATE for 15 minutes. Preheat oven to 400°F (200°C).

BAKE for 20 to 25 minutes or until scones are golden.

×

Apple and Cheddar Sandwich

—

1 Cortland apple

1 Granny Smith apple

Juice of 1 lemon

6 mint leaves, chopped

1 tablespoon (15 mL) olive oil

4 slices toast

4 thick slices sharp or extra-sharp Cheddar cheese

6 chives, chopped

1 cup (250 mL) arugula or watercress

—

CUT apples into thin slices with a mandoline or knife. Toss with lemon juice and sprinkle with mint.

DRIZZLE olive oil on toast. Arrange cheese and apple slices on 2 pieces of toast.

GARNISH with chives and arugula. Close sandwiches and serve.

×

Beautiful Renée's Vegetable Spread

2 onions, cut into chunks

1 carrot, cut into chunks

1 celery stalk, cut into chunks

1 potato, grated

1 cup (250 mL) hot water

¾ cup (180 mL) unbleached all-purpose flour

⅓ cup (160 mL) nutritional yeast (see below)

½ cup (125 mL) sunflower seeds

⅓ cup (80 mL) olive oil

¼ cup (60 mL) tamari

2 tablespoons (30 mL) lemon juice

1 garlic clove, minced

Leaves from 2 thyme sprigs, chopped

2 sage leaves, chopped

Nutritional yeast

An important source of protein and vitamins (especially B), this yeast has a slight cheesy tang. It is found in health food stores.

PREHEAT oven to 350°F (180°C).

COMBINE onions, carrot and celery in a food processor until finely chopped. Transfer to a large bowl.

ADD remaining ingredients and mix to form a paste.

SPREAD about 1½ inches (4 cm) thick in a 9-inch (2.5 L) square baking dish. Bake for 45 minutes or until mixture has firmed up slightly. Cool completely, then unmould.

SERVE in sandwiches with greens and pickled vegetables, if desired. The spread freezes well.

×

Tofu Schnitzel Sandwich

Marinade

2 garlic cloves, peeled

2 inches (5 cm) fresh ginger, peeled

¼ cup (60 mL) natural apple juice

3 tablespoons (45 mL) olive oil

2 tablespoons (30 mL) brown rice miso paste

Sandwich

½ lb (225 g) block organic firm tofu

Sea salt and freshly cracked pepper

½ cup (125 mL) unbleached all-purpose flour

2 eggs

1 cup (250 mL) toasted sesame seeds

½ cup (125 mL) olive or vegetable oil

4 ciabatta buns, halved

Marinated mushrooms, roasted peppers, artichoke hearts or other antipasti

1 cup (250 mL) frisée or other lettuce

PURÉE garlic and ginger in a food processor. Add apple juice, oil and miso; pulse to combine. Pour marinade into a baking dish large enough to hold the tofu slices in one layer.

CUT tofu into ½-inch (1 cm) slices. Season. Place in the dish with marinade, turn to coat well and refrigerate for 2 hours.

PLACE flour in a shallow dish and season with salt and pepper. Beat eggs in another shallow dish. Place sesame seeds in a third dish. Pat tofu slices with paper towel. Dredge slices in flour, then in eggs and finally in sesame seeds.

HEAT oil in a skillet over medium-high heat. Fry tofu slices for 3 to 4 minutes per side or until golden. Drain on paper towel.

PLACE tofu schnitzel in ciabatta buns. Garnish with marinated vegetables and lettuce. Cover with the other half of the bun.

×

Ham and Butter Sandwich (Jambon-Beurre)

½ baguette

1 tablespoon (15 mL) cold salted or unsalted butter (cold tastes better)

4 to 6 slices ham

4 cornichons

6 chives, chopped

1 tomato, sliced

2 to 4 leaves romaine lettuce

SLICE baguette lengthwise and spread with butter.

PLACE ham slices in baguette and top with remaining ingredients.

×

Serves 4

Ham Salad Tartine

7 oz (200 g) ham

2 celery stalks, chopped

1 endive, chopped

2 tablespoons (30 mL) chopped walnuts

6 chives, chopped

¼ cup (60 mL) chopped flat-leaf parsley

½ cup (125 mL) mayonnaise

Sea salt and freshly cracked pepper

4 lettuce leaves, chopped

4 slices whole wheat bread

CHOP ham and place in a medium bowl.

STIR in remaining ingredients except lettuce and bread. Season.

SPREAD ham salad on bread. Garnish with lettuce.

×

Prosciutto Sandwich

—

1 fennel bulb, cut
lengthwise into ½-inch
(1 cm) slices

Juice of 1 lemon

2 tablespoons (30 mL)
olive oil

3 tablespoons (45 mL)
grated Parmesan cheese

12 slices prosciutto

1 cup (250 mL) arugula

12 basil leaves

2 tomatoes, sliced

8 slices bread
(or 4 ciabatta buns)

Sea salt and freshly
cracked pepper

—

Variations

You can replace the
tomatoes with figs or
nectarine slices.

You can replace roasted
Parmesan fennel with
fennel salad (p. 129).

—

PREHEAT oven to 400°F (200°C).

PLACE fennel slices on a baking sheet.
Drizzle with lemon juice and oil.
Sprinkle with Parmesan.

COVER with foil and bake for 20 minutes.
Uncover and continue cooking for
5 minutes or until golden.

ARRANGE prosciutto, fennel, arugula, basil
and tomatoes on bread slices. Season.

×

Tandoori Chicken Sandwich

—

1 lb (500 g) boneless, skinless chicken thighs

1 beet, puréed in a food processor

Juice of 1 lemon

1½ teaspoons (7 mL) grated fresh ginger

1½ teaspoons (7 mL) minced garlic + 1 garlic clove, chopped

1 cup (250 mL) + ¼ cup (60 mL) 10% yogurt

2 tablespoons (30 mL) garam masala

Sea salt and freshly cracked pepper

4 naan breads or pitas

1 mini or Lebanese cucumber, thinly sliced

8 to 10 mint leaves, chopped

½ to 1 cup (125 to 250 mL) coarsely chopped cilantro

—

Variations

You can serve tandoori chicken with a mint and coriander sauce and a mango or pineapple salad. Or with grilled vegetables.

—

CUT chicken into bite-size pieces. Add beet purée, lemon juice, ginger and minced garlic. Cover and refrigerate for 1 hour.

ADD 1 cup (250 mL) yogurt and garam masala. Season. Cover and refrigerate for another 4 hours.

PREHEAT grill or oven to 400°F (200°C). Soak wooden skewers for 30 minutes.

THREAD chicken pieces onto skewers. Grill for 10 to 15 minutes or bake on a baking sheet for 15 to 20 minutes.

MIX remaining ¼ cup (60 mL) yogurt and chopped garlic in a small bowl and let stand for 10 minutes.

PILE chicken onto naans. Garnish with cucumber, herbs and yogurt sauce.

×

Italian Chicken Ciabatta

½ boneless, skinless chicken breast

½ cup (125 mL) unbleached all-purpose flour

Sea salt and freshly cracked pepper

3 eggs

1 cup (250 mL) dry bread crumbs

Leaves from 4 oregano sprigs, chopped

½ cup (125 mL) olive or vegetable oil

1 tablespoon (15 mL) mayonnaise

1 teaspoon (5 mL) basil pesto (or ½ teaspoon/2 mL minced chipotle in adobo sauce; see p. 240)

2 ciabatta buns, halved

1 to 2 tomatoes, sliced

Roasted peppers, marinated eggplant or other antipasti

1 cup (250 mL) arugula

CUT chicken in half horizontally. Pound between sheets of plastic wrap to about ½-inch (1 cm) thickness.

ADD flour to a shallow dish and season with salt and pepper. Beat eggs in another shallow dish. Combine bread crumbs and oregano in a third dish. Dredge chicken in flour, then in eggs and finally in bread crumbs.

HEAT oil in a large skillet over medium-high heat. Fry chicken pieces until cooked through and golden on both sides. Drain on paper towel.

COMBINE mayonnaise and pesto in a small bowl. Spread on bread.

PLACE chicken on ciabattas. Top with tomato slices and marinated vegetables. Add a few leaves of arugula and cover with the other half of the bun.

×

Curried Chicken Sandwich

224

—

2 cups (500 mL)
diced cooked chicken

1 red onion, minced

1 celery stalk, finely diced

3 radishes, thinly sliced

1 green apple, unpeeled,
diced

¼ cup (60 mL) currants

¼ cup (60 mL) sour cream
or yogurt

¼ cup (60 mL) mayonnaise

1 tablespoon (15 mL)
Madras curry powder

1 tablespoon (15 mL) honey

8 slices bread, 4 pitas
or 4 tortillas

1 cup (250 mL) arugula
or watercress

—

MIX all ingredients, except bread and arugula, in a large bowl.

TOP bread with chicken mixture and greens.

×

Serves 2

Merguez Sandwich

—

½ baguette

1 to 2 teaspoons (5 to 10 mL) Dijon mustard

4 grilled Merguez sausages

½ cup (125 mL) coleslaw (p. 120)

—

SLICE baguette lengthwise and scoop out some bread from the centre. Spread baguette with mustard.

TOP each half with sausages and coleslaw.

×

Serves 2

Duck Sandwich

—

1 tablespoon (15 mL) olive oil, plus extra for drizzling

¼ leek, white part only, cut into matchsticks

2 pitas

1 confit duck leg, skin removed and meat shredded

½ mango, sliced

Sea salt and freshly cracked pepper

A few basil leaves

A few arugula leaves

Balsamic vinegar reduction (p. 206)

—

Variations

The mango can be replaced with a green apple cut into matchsticks or slices of fig.

—

HEAT 1 tbsp (15 mL) oil in a skillet over medium-low heat. Sauté leek for 2 to 3 minutes with 1 tbsp (15 mL) water. Remove from heat.

DRIZZLE oil on pitas. Top with duck, mango and leek.

SEASON and garnish with basil, arugula and balsamic reduction.

×

Sloppy Joes

—

2 tablespoons (30 mL) olive oil

2 lb (1 kg) ground beef

2 onions, chopped

2 carrots, very finely chopped

1 tablespoon (15 mL) ground cumin + 2 tablespoons (30 mL) chili powder + ½ teaspoon (2 mL) cayenne

1 tablespoon (15 mL) chopped oregano

2 garlic cloves, chopped

1 can (14 oz/398 mL) diced tomatoes, drained

3 tablespoons (45 mL) tomato paste

1 tablespoon (15 mL) Worcestershire sauce

Sea salt and freshly cracked pepper

4 hamburger buns, toasted

½ cup (125 mL) grated medium yellow Cheddar cheese

1 cup (250 mL) chopped cilantro or flat-leaf parsley

—

HEAT oil in a large skillet over medium-high heat. Brown meat, onions and carrots for 5 to 7 minutes.

ADD spices and oregano. Cook for 2 to 3 minutes or until meat is no longer pink.

STIR in garlic, tomatoes, tomato paste and Worcestershire sauce. Bring to a boil, then reduce heat and simmer for 10 minutes or until thickened. Season.

SERVE in buns and top with cheese and cilantro.

×

Genoa Salami Sandwich

—

2 tablespoons (30 mL) mayonnaise

½ teaspoon (2 mL) minced chipotle in adobo sauce (see p. 240) or 1 teaspoon (5 mL) basil pesto

2 ciabatta buns (or ½ baguette), halved

15 thin slices Genoa salami

1 roasted sweet red pepper, cut into strips

1 tomato, sliced

2 tablespoons (30 mL) caramelized onions (see below)

½ cup (125 mL) arugula or other lettuce

—

Caramelized Onions

Heat 3 tbsp (45 mL) butter or olive oil in a large skillet over medium-high heat. Add 2 cups (500 mL) finely chopped onions. Sauté for 3 to 5 minutes, stirring often, then reduce heat to low and cook for 30 minutes or until golden brown. Caramelized onions will keep for up to 2 weeks in the refrigerator.

—

COMBINE mayonnaise and chipotle in a small bowl. Spread onto bread.

TOP with salami slices. Garnish with roasted pepper, sliced tomato, caramelized onions and greens.

×

Ragù Sandwich

—

2 balls bocconcini, sliced

2 panini buns, slit open lengthwise

½ to 1 cup (125 to 250 mL) hot ragù sauce (see opposite)

10 basil leaves

¼ cup (60 mL) arugula

—

PREHEAT broiler.

PAT bocconcini with paper towel to remove any excess moisture.

LAY bocconcini inside bread and broil until cheese melts.

OPEN bread carefully and top with sauce. Garnish with basil and arugula.

×

Ragù Sauce

—

2 tablespoons (30 mL) butter

¼ cup (60 mL) olive oil

1 oz (30 g) pancetta or speck, diced

1 medium carrot, finely diced

1 celery stalk, finely diced

1 onion, finely chopped

3 garlic cloves, chopped

1 cup (250 mL) diced mushrooms

1 lb (500 g) ground pork or beef

1 lb (500 g) ground veal

Sea salt and freshly cracked pepper

1 cup (250 mL) white wine

5 cups (1.25 L) diced tomatoes (fresh or canned)

1 tablespoon (15 mL) chopped oregano or a branch of dried

1 cup (250 mL) milk

1 small chili pepper, seeded and diced

—

HEAT butter and olive oil in a large saucepan over medium heat. Cook pancetta for 2 minutes.

ADD carrot, celery, onion and garlic. Cook for 10 minutes or until tender.

ADD mushrooms. Cook for 3 minutes.

STIR in pork and veal. Season. Cook for 10 minutes, stirring occasionally.

ADD wine, tomatoes and oregano. Bring to a boil. Reduce heat to low and simmer, uncovered, for 1 hour.

ADD milk and chili pepper. Cook for another 30 minutes.

REFRIGERATE overnight and serve ragù sauce the next day, over pasta or in sandwiches (see opposite).

×

Tuna Sandwich

—

2 cans (6 oz/170 g each)
tuna in oil or water, drained

Zest (optional) and juice of
1 organic lemon

½ small red onion, minced

2 tablespoons (30 mL)
chopped fresh herbs of
your choice

1 tablespoon (15 mL) capers

½ cup (125 mL) mayonnaise

4 sesame seed buns, halved

Sea salt and freshly
cracked pepper

12 cherry tomatoes, halved

½ package (4 oz/114 g)
alfalfa or other sprouts

—

PLACE tuna in a bowl. Add lemon juice
(and zest, if desired), onion, herbs,
capers and mayonnaise. Stir with a
fork to combine.

SPREAD half the bread with tuna mixture.
Season. Top with tomatoes and alfalfa.
Cover with the other halves of buns.

×

—

Greek-Style
Tuna Sandwich

Mix 2 cans of drained tuna
with 2 tbsp (30 mL) chopped
feta (not too salty) and
¼ cup (60 mL) mayonnaise.
Add 8 pitted, quartered
Kalamata olives, ½ cup
(125 mL) coarsely chopped
flat-leaf parsley, ½ small
red onion, chopped, and
chopped leaves from
4 oregano sprigs.

—

Indian-Style
Tuna Sandwich

Use the ingredients for the
tandoori chicken sandwich
recipe (p. 222), with drained
tuna in place of chicken.

Cuban Shrimp Tartine

—

2 tablespoons (30 mL) olive oil

3 garlic cloves, chopped

1 small onion, chopped

2 cups (500 mL) cooked black beans

1½ teaspoons (7 mL) finely chopped chipotle in adobo sauce (see p. 240)

1 teaspoon (5 mL) ground cumin

Sea salt and freshly cracked pepper

Juice of 1 to 2 limes

8 to 12 medium shrimp, peeled

A pinch of smoked paprika

4 slices cornbread, toasted

1 cup (250 mL) mango salsa (see below)

½ cup (125 mL) cooked corn kernels (frozen or fresh, see p. 152)

—

Mango Salsa

Dice 1 large mango, 2 medium tomatoes and ½ to 1 avocado. Sprinkle with a pinch of cayenne, the juice of ½ lime and 1 tbsp (15 mL) olive oil. Stir in ½ cup (125 mL) chopped cilantro and season. Let stand at room temperature for 10 minutes.

HEAT 1 tbsp (15 mL) oil in a large skillet over medium heat. Add 2 cloves of garlic and onion; sauté for 3 minutes to soften.

ADD black beans, chipotle and cumin. Season. Cook for 2 minutes, stirring often. Remove from heat.

SQUEEZE in lime juice to taste. Mash bean mixture with a potato masher. Reserve.

HEAT 1 tbsp (15 mL) oil in a separate skillet over medium-high heat. Sauté shrimp with remaining garlic and smoked paprika, without turning, for 2 minutes, then flip and cook another minute. Remove from heat and top with a dash of lime juice.

SPREAD bread slices with mashed black beans. Top with salsa, corn and shrimp.

×

Smoked Salmon Tartine

—

¼ lb (125 g) smoked salmon or smoked trout, cut into large strips

1 Granny Smith apple, cut into matchsticks

1 celery stalk, minced

6 chives, chopped

1 tablespoon (15 mL) capers

⅓ cup (80 mL) sour cream

⅓ cup (80 mL) mayonnaise

Juice of ½ lemon

Sea salt and freshly cracked pepper

2 slices rye bread

A few dill or fennel fronds

—

COMBINE salmon, apple, celery, chives and capers in a large bowl.

MIX sour cream, mayonnaise and lemon juice in a small bowl. Pour sour cream mixture over salmon and mix. Season.

SPOON over rye bread and garnish with dill or fennel.

×

Lobster Roll

—

2 medium lobsters,
cooked and shelled

½ cup (125 mL) mayonnaise

1 celery stalk, finely
chopped

Zest and juice of
1 organic lemon

Sea salt and freshly
cracked pepper

Leaves from 3 tarragon
sprigs, chopped

6 chives, chopped

4 hotdog buns

1 tablespoon (15 mL) butter

4 leaves Bibb lettuce

—

Variation

Replace the lobster
with crabmeat.

—

CHOP lobster meat into large pieces. Combine lobster, mayonnaise, celery, lemon juice and lemon zest in a large bowl. Season and mix with a fork.

STIR in tarragon and chives.

BUTTER both sides of hotdog buns and toast in a pan until golden.

PLACE a lettuce leaf inside each bun and fill with lobster mixture. Eat with your eyes closed!

×

Lobster BLT

—

1 lobster, cooked
and shelled

1 tablespoon (15 mL)
butter, melted

8 chives, chopped

Juice of ½ lemon

¼ cup (60 mL) mayonnaise

1 teaspoon (5 mL) minced
chipotle in adobo sauce
(see below) or a pinch of
smoked paprika

8 slices bread

8 slices cooked bacon

2 tomatoes, sliced

4 leaves romaine lettuce

Sea salt and freshly
cracked pepper

—

Chipotles in adobo
sauce

These small smoked
jalapeños are canned in a
red wine vinegar sauce.

—

MIX lobster meat in a bowl along with melted butter and chives. Squeeze lemon juice on top and reserve.

COMBINE mayonnaise and chipotle in a small bowl. Spread over bread slices.

TOP with lobster, bacon, tomatoes and lettuce. Season and close sandwiches.

×

Crab Cakes

—

1 cup (250 mL) shredded crabmeat

½ cup (125 mL) corn kernels
(frozen or fresh, see p. 152)

½ cup (125 mL) finely chopped
cilantro

1 teaspoon (5 mL) finely chopped
red chili pepper

1 green onion, finely chopped

1 celery stalk, finely chopped

2 tablespoons (30 mL) mayonnaise

Zest and juice of ½ organic lime

2 to 3 tablespoons
(30 to 45 mL) + 1 cup
(250 mL) dry bread crumbs

Sea salt and freshly cracked pepper

1 cup (250 mL) unbleached
all-purpose flour

3 eggs, beaten

1 cup (250 mL) canola or olive oil

—

Pineapple Salsa

Combine a pineapple, cut into
cubes, 1 cup (250 mL) quartered
cherry tomatoes and ½ sweet
red pepper, cubanelle or poblano
chili, diced. Add 1 green onion,
sliced on the diagonal, and 1 red
chili pepper, seeded and finely
chopped. Drizzle with the juice of
1 to 2 limes and 1 tbsp (15 mL)
olive oil. Stir in 1 cup (250 mL)
chopped cilantro and season.
Marinate in refrigerator for 1 hour.

—

PLACE first 7 ingredients in a bowl
and mix. Stir in lime zest and juice.
Add 2 to 3 tbsp (30 to 45 mL) bread
crumbs to ensure that the mixture is
not too moist. Season.

FORM 4 to 6 patties and place on a
baking sheet. Refrigerate for 1 hour.

DREDGE patties in flour. Dip in beaten
eggs, then dredge in remaining
bread crumbs.

HEAT oil in a deep skillet over
medium-high heat. Gently place
patties in skillet. Fry for 2 to 3 minutes,
flip and cook for another minute.
Drain on paper towel.

SERVE crab cakes accompanied by
mango salsa (p. 234) or pineapple
salsa (see below).

×

Desserts

Chocolate Dessert Soup with Saffron and Chili

—

6 tablespoons (90 mL)
35% (whipping) cream

2 pinches of saffron

2 pinches of
red pepper flakes

1 cup (250 mL)
70% chocolate cut into
small pieces

6 tablespoons (90 mL)
whole (homogenized) milk,
warmed

—

HEAT cream, a pinch of saffron and a pinch of red pepper flakes in a small saucepan over medium heat. Simmer for 5 minutes.

PLACE chocolate in a bowl. Pour in hot infused cream. Stir to melt chocolate.

ADD warm milk as needed if the soup is too thick.

DIVIDE among 4 small espresso cups. Garnish with a pinch of saffron and red pepper flakes.

×

Coconut Crumble

—

½ cup (125 mL) unbleached all-purpose flour

½ cup (125 mL) brown sugar

½ cup (125 mL) shredded unsweetened coconut

¼ cup (60 mL) cold butter, cut into small pieces

3 mangoes, cut into pieces

½ pineapple, cut into pieces

—

PREHEAT oven to 375°F (190°C).

COMBINE flour, brown sugar and coconut in a large bowl. Rub in butter by hand.

PLACE fruit in a 9-inch (2.5 L) square baking dish and cover with coconut topping. Bake for 20 to 25 minutes, until top is golden and fruit is bubbling.

×

Berry Crumble

—

3 cups (750 mL) large-flake rolled oats

1½ cups (375 mL) unbleached all-purpose flour

1½ cups (375 mL) brown sugar

½ lb (225 g) cold butter, cut into small pieces

3 cups (750 mL) mixed berries

—

—

PREHEAT oven to 375°F (190°C).

COMBINE oats, flour and brown sugar in a large bowl. Rub in butter by hand.

PLACE berries in a 13- by 9-inch (3 L) baking dish and cover with oat mixture. Bake for 25 to 30 minutes, until top is golden and fruit is bubbling.

×

Variations

Some other winning combinations: raspberry and mango, strawberries and rhubarb, blueberry and pear, apple and cranberry.

Jasmine Pears

—

4 cups (1 L) water

2 jasmine tea bags

¾ inch (2 cm) fresh ginger

1 small cinnamon stick

1 star anise

1 tablespoon (15 mL)
goji berries

4 pears, peeled, cut in half
and cored

¼ cup (60 mL) cane sugar

—

BOIL water in a saucepan. Add tea, reduce heat and infuse for 10 minutes, then remove tea bags.

ADD ginger, cinnamon, star anise and goji berries to tea.

PLACE a rack on the bottom of the saucepan, add pears and poach in tea for 15 to 20 minutes or until tender.

REMOVE pears and place in serving bowls. Strain tea and return to pot.

ADD sugar to tea and reduce over high heat for 5 minutes. Pour over pears.

×

Lemon Cake

—

½ cup (125 mL) butter

1 cup (250 mL) cane sugar

Zest of 1 organic lemon

3 eggs

1 cup (250 mL) unbleached
all-purpose flour

1 teaspoon (5 mL)
baking powder

½ cup (125 mL) yogurt

—

PREHEAT oven to 350°F (180°C). Butter and flour a 9-inch (23 cm) square or round cake pan.

BEAT butter with an electric mixer until creamy. Add sugar and zest; beat for 3 minutes. Add eggs 1 at a time, beating after each addition.

COMBINE flour and baking powder. Fold into batter. Add yogurt and mix until just combined.

POUR batter into prepared pan. Bake for 30 minutes or until a toothpick inserted in centre comes out clean.

COOL for 10 minutes before unmoulding.

×

Trifle

—

2 cups (500 mL)
strawberries, halved

¼ cup (60 mL)
+ 3 tablespoons (45 mL)
cane sugar

2 cups (500 mL)
35% cream, chilled

Zest and juice of
1 organic lemon

1 lemon cake, cut into
cubes (p. 256)

—

PLACE strawberries and ¼ cup (60 mL) sugar in a bowl. Mix gently and reserve.

WHIP cream with remaining 3 tbsp (45 mL) sugar in a chilled bowl until soft peaks form. Whisk in lemon zest and juice.

PLACE a little lemon whipped cream in a large glass bowl, add some pieces of cake, then strawberries and their juice. Continue alternating layers, finishing with a layer of strawberries.

COVER with plastic wrap and refrigerate until ready to serve.

×

Cardamom Brownies

—

7 medium eggs

1¼ cups (310 mL) cane sugar

⅔ cup (160 mL) butter

½ cup (125 mL) + 2 tablespoons (30 mL) 70% chocolate chips

½ cup (125 mL) cocoa powder

⅓ cup (80 mL) unbleached all-purpose flour

½ to 1 teaspoon (2 to 5 mL) ground cardamom (or 2 pinches of cayenne)

—

PREHEAT oven to 350°F (180°C). Line the bottom of a 9-inch (23 cm) square cake pan with parchment paper.

WHISK eggs with sugar in a large bowl.

MELT butter and ½ cup (125 mL) chocolate in a microwave or over a double boiler. Stir into egg mixture.

COMBINE cocoa and flour. Stir into wet ingredients. Stir in cardamom.

POUR into prepared pan and sprinkle with remaining 2 tbsp (30 mL) chocolate chips. Bake for 20 to 25 minutes or until top of cake springs back when touched.

×

Chocolate Panna Cotta

—

2 gelatin sheets

2 cups (500 mL) 35% cream

1¾ oz (50 g) cane sugar

3½ oz (100 g)
70% chocolate chips

—

Variations

Replace the chocolate with different flavours. Steep hot sweetened cream for 15 minutes with any of the following before straining: lemon (zest of ½ organic lemon), tea (1 bag), anise (1 star anise), ginger (1 tbsp grated), lavender (1 tsp).

—

SOAK gelatin in a bowl of cold water. Drain and squeeze out any excess water.

BRING cream and sugar to a boil in a saucepan. Remove from heat, add chocolate chips and stir until melted.

ADD gelatin to hot cream and mix well.

POUR mixture into 4 ramekins and refrigerate for at least 6 hours. Top with berry salad (see below) or a few pistachios.

×

Berry Salad

—

¼ cup (60 mL) agave nectar

3 to 4 lemon verbena leaves

1 cup (250 mL) strawberries, cut into pieces

1 cup (250 mL) blueberries

1 cup (250 mL) blackberries

Juice of 1 lime

—

SIMMER agave nectar in a saucepan. Add verbena leaves and simmer for 5 more minutes. Remove from heat. Let stand for 15 minutes, then remove leaves.

PLACE all fruit in a bowl, add the syrup and lime juice, and stir gently to mix.

×

—

<u>Variations</u>

**Replace the lemon verbena
with basil, mint or a little
rosemary.**

Lemon Squares

Pastry

½ lb (225 g) cold butter

2 cups (500 mL) unbleached all-purpose flour

½ cup (125 mL) cane sugar

½ teaspoon (2 mL) sea salt

Filling

6 eggs

2 cups (500 mL) cane sugar

1 cup (250 mL) lemon juice

Zest of 2 organic lemons (optional)

1 cup (250 mL) unbleached all-purpose flour, sifted

Icing sugar

Variation

Replace the lemon juice and zest with lime juice and zest.

PREHEAT oven to 350°F (180°C). Line the bottom of a 13- by 9-inch (3 L) baking dish with parchment paper.

PULSE butter with the flour, sugar and salt in a food processor, or blend with your fingertips, until it resembles bread crumbs.

PRESS mixture into the bottom of the baking dish. Bake for 15 minutes; do not let brown. Let cool.

BEAT eggs, sugar, lemon juice and zest, if desired, in a bowl using a whisk. Sift flour over the bowl while whisking to prevent lumps.

POUR filling over crust. Bake for 15 to 20 minutes, until filling is almost set.

REFRIGERATE. Cut while cold into squares and dust with icing sugar.

×

Raspberry Scones

—

1½ cups (375 mL)
fresh or frozen (unthawed)
raspberries

2 eggs

¾ cup (180 mL) milk

Juice of 1 lemon

4 cups (1 L) unbleached
all-purpose flour

1 teaspoon (5 mL)
baking powder

1 teaspoon (5 mL)
baking soda

1 cup (250 mL) sugar

1¼ cups (310 mL) cold
butter, cut into pieces

—

Freezing scones

Simply place the tray of
unbaked scones in the
freezer for 2 hours, then
transfer scones to a
freezer bag. You can bake
the scones directly from the
freezer whenever you
want one!

—

FREEZE fresh raspberries for 30 minutes to prevent them from getting crushed in the dough.

BEAT eggs with milk in a small bowl. Add lemon juice and let stand for 4 minutes.

COMBINE all dry ingredients with the butter in a food processor until mixture resembles bread crumbs.

ADD egg mixture and pulse until dough is just combined. Transfer dough to a large bowl.

FORM dough into 12 patties. Using your fingers, push raspberries into each scone. Place on a parchment-lined baking sheet.

REFRIGERATE for 15 minutes. Preheat oven to 400°F (200°C).

BAKE for 20 to 25 minutes. Because raspberries tend to release a lot of liquid, these scones may require more cooking time at a reduced oven temperature of 350°F (180°C). Stack two baking sheets together to prevent burning the scones.

×

Strawberry Shortcakes

—

Dough for raspberry scones, without fruit (p. 263)

2 cups (500 mL) strawberries

3 tablespoons (45 mL) cane sugar

Ginger whipped cream (see below)

—

Variations

Replace ginger whipped cream with lemon-flavoured whipped cream (Trifle, p. 258).

For a lighter version, replace whipped cream with yogurt.

—

FLATTEN dough with your fist until it is about ¾ inch (2 cm) thick.

CUT out circles of dough using the rim of a small glass as a cutter. Place on a parchment-lined baking sheet and freeze for 15 minutes.

PREHEAT oven to 400°F (200°C).

CUT strawberries into halves or thirds. Place in a bowl, sprinkle with sugar and toss lightly. Macerate for 20 minutes.

BAKE shortcakes for 12 to 15 minutes.

OPEN cakes horizontally. fill with strawberries and ginger whipped cream.

×

Ginger Whipped Cream

—

2 cups (500 mL) 35% cream (or a mixture of 1 cup/ 250 mL 35% cream and 1 cup/250 mL mascarpone)

3 tablespoons (45 mL) finely chopped candied ginger

—

WHIP cream with electric mixer until firm peaks form.

FOLD in candied ginger.

REFRIGERATE for 30 minutes.

×

Pudding Chômeur

—

2 cups (500 mL) unbleached all-purpose flour

2 teaspoons (10 mL) baking powder

A pinch of salt

½ cup (125 mL) butter, at room temperature

1 cup (250 mL) cane sugar

2 eggs

½ cup (125 mL) milk

2¼ cups (550 mL) maple syrup

2 cups (500 mL) 35% cream

—

Note

Watch out—it is not uncommon for pudding cakes to overflow in the oven. Place a baking sheet on a rack underneath to catch the damage.

You can also make a bit more sauce and reserve some to drizzle on top before serving.

—

PREHEAT oven to 400°F (200°C).

COMBINE flour, baking powder and salt in a small bowl.

BEAT butter and sugar with an electric mixer in a large bowl for 2 to 3 minutes or until light and creamy. Add eggs and beat for another minute.

BEAT in dry ingredients alternately with milk. Pour into a 13- by 9-inch (3 L) cake pan.

BOIL maple syrup and cream in a large saucepan for 3 to 4 minutes.

POUR boiling maple syrup mixture over batter. Bake for 30 minutes or until a toothpick inserted in the centre of the cake comes out clean. Serve warm.

×

Rice Pudding

4 cups (1 L) milk or soy milk

¾ cup (180 mL) arborio rice

1 cinnamon stick

½ cup (125 mL) cane sugar

2 egg yolks

1 tablespoon (15 mL) rose water

1 pomegranate, seeded (or 1 cup/250 mL mixed berries)

BUTTER 4 to 6 ramekins.

BRING milk to a boil. Add rice and cinnamon stick. Reduce heat to a simmer and cook for 20 minutes or until all the liquid is absorbed and the rice is cooked through. Remove the cinnamon stick.

REMOVE from heat and add sugar.

BEAT egg yolks with rose water. Using a spatula, fold the mixture into the rice.

DIVIDE pudding among ramekins and refrigerate for 6 hours. Unmould and garnish with pomegranate seeds.

×

Peanut Butter Cookies

—

½ lb (225 g) butter, softened

1 cup (250 mL) cane sugar

1 cup (250 mL) brown sugar

2 eggs

2½ cups (625 mL)
unbleached all-purpose flour

1 teaspoon (5 mL)
baking soda

1½ cups (375 mL)
natural peanut butter

½ cup (125 mL)
coarsely chopped peanuts
(optional)

—

PREHEAT oven to 325°F (160°C).

BEAT butter, cane sugar and brown
sugar together using an electric mixer for
3 to 4 minutes or until mixture is light
and fluffy.

ADD eggs and continue beating. Mix
together flour and baking soda. Add to
batter along with peanut butter. Stir until
batter is smooth.

FORM into balls, place on a parchment-
lined baking sheet and press flat.
Sprinkle with chopped peanuts,
if desired. Refrigerate for 30 minutes.

BAKE for 10 to 12 minutes or until cookies
are golden yet still soft. They will harden
as they cool, but should still be soft the
next day.

×

Cranberry and Chocolate Oatmeal Cookies

¾ cup (180 mL) cane sugar

¾ cup (180 mL) brown sugar

½ lb (225 g) butter, softened

2 eggs

1 cup (250 mL) unbleached all-purpose flour

1 teaspoon (5 mL) baking powder

1 teaspoon (5 mL) baking soda

1 teaspoon (5 mL) salt

4 cups (1 L) large-flake rolled oats

½ cup (125 mL) 70% chocolate chips

½ cup (125 mL) dried cranberries

—

Variation

Pecans go very well with this recipe. You can add ⅓ cup (80 mL) pecans cut into halves or thirds and press into the tops of the cookies just before baking.

PREHEAT oven to 350°F (180°C).

BEAT cane sugar, brown sugar and butter in a bowl. Beat in eggs.

MIX together flour, baking powder, baking soda, salt and oats. Stir into sugar mixture. Stir in chocolate and cranberries and mix well.

FORM into balls, place on a parchment-lined baking sheet and flatten slightly. Refrigerate for 30 minutes.

BAKE for 10 to 12 minutes or until cookies are golden yet still soft. They will harden as they cool, but should still be soft the next day.

×

Ginger Cookies

—

3 tablespoons (45 mL) grated fresh ginger

½ cup (125 mL) canola oil

2 eggs

1 cup (250 mL) cane sugar

¼ cup (60 mL) molasses

2¼ cups (560 mL) unbleached all-purpose flour

1 teaspoon (5 mL) cinnamon

1 teaspoon (5 mL) baking soda

½ teaspoon (2 mL) baking powder

A pinch of cayenne

A pinch of ground cloves

A pinch of sea salt

—

Note

You can roll out the dough and cut into cookies using a cookie cutter. Or form dough into a log, wrap carefully with plastic wrap and freeze, then slice into cookies.

—

PREHEAT oven to 325°F (160°C).

PLACE ginger and oil in a small bowl. Macerate for 10 minutes, then strain, if desired, to remove any fibrous bits of ginger. Reserve ginger and infused oil.

BEAT eggs with sugar and molasses in a large bowl. Add oil and ginger and mix well.

COMBINE all dry ingredients. Add to batter and mix until smooth. Refrigerate for 30 minutes.

FORM dough into balls, place on a parchment-lined baking sheet and press flat.

BAKE for about 9 minutes.

×

PROVOLONE

— FRIULANO

Pancetta 9/

GENOA

— DINDE 2½/3

— Chèvre ⎤ petite
　　Boursin ⎦

— Hummus ⎤ GROS

Some of the basics . . .

Fruits and vegetables

With the vast selection of fruits and vegetables available, I just love incorporating as many fresh varieties into my recipes as possible. The exciting part is, when you let yourself be guided by what is fresh at the market, you end up making new discoveries along the way! With soup, in particular, I make sure to incorporate each vegetable at the right time and not to overcook them, so as to preserve their flavour, texture, colour and all their nutritional properties.

Legumes

If you can, try to cook them yourself. When you season them with a bay leaf, sage or a few sprigs of thyme, and a pinch of salt right at the end, legumes have much more flavour and are much more digestible than those found in a can. You can always cook them in advance and freeze for whenever you need them.

Spices

For more intense flavour, I prefer non-ground spices and either leave them whole or grind them at the very last minute. To deepen their flavour, roast them in a dry skillet for 3 minutes before grinding.

Lemon and lime

Loaded with vitamins, these will subtly enhance any recipe. I don't know what I would do without them . . . When a recipe calls for zest, I prefer using organic citrus. If you don't have any organic fruit on hand, be sure to wash the fruit several times in water (no soap!).

You can also substitute lemon juice for lime, orange, or grapefruit juice.

Fresh Herb Coulis

1 cup (250 mL) basil (or one of the herbal blends opposite)

¼ cup (60 mL) olive oil

1 teaspoon (5 mL) sea salt

1 teaspoon (5 mL) raw sugar

Juice of ½ lemon

PURÉE all ingredients in a blender for ½ cup (125 mL) of coulis that you can use to garnish soups, sandwiches and salads. You can also use it to flavour a salad dressing or mayonnaise. By adding chopped nuts and grated Parmesan cheese, you get a pesto.

×

—

Fresh herbs

I almost always use fresh herbs; they add colour and flavour to soups, sandwiches and salads. In fact, I find that it is better to replace basil with fresh flat-leaf parsley or fresh oregano than to use dried basil. I really encourage you to try different fresh herbs and to discover the ones you like best. Fresh herbs are much less pungent than dried herbs, so you won't risk ruining your recipe.

Place fresh herbs in a bag or an airtight container after you remove them from the bouquet. Depending on the humidity in your refrigerator, you can extend the shelf life of certain herbs like parsley, chives and cilantro by rolling them in a damp paper towel before packaging. Sage, thyme and rosemary, however, do not need the moisture.

When you have leftover herbs, consider making a herb and lettuce salad with a lemon vinaigrette—they are richer in vitamins than many vegetables. You could also try making fresh tea—it's so much better than using a bag—or simply make a herb coulis (see opposite). Freeze the finished coulis in small freezer bags (very handy!) to have fresh coulis whenever you need it.

—

Fresh herb blends

Use the fresh herbs that are in your refrigerator before they spoil. Here are some suggestions for delicious combinations:

Basil, mint and coriander

Mint, cilantro and chives

Tarragon and basil

—

Ideas for using fresh herbs:

Basil: **A classic with tomatoes. You can also incorporate basil into almost any salad, even fruit salads.**

Cilantro: **Can be used in all Asian and Indian dishes, and also with tabbouleh and lamb. Coriander can reveal very interesting tastes when paired with other fresh herbs.**

Parsley: **It is often forgotten, and while its scent may be discreet, it certainly adds a lot of freshness. Rediscover it in Italian dishes, with beans, meat (beef, ham) or shrimp.**

Celery leaves: **Do not throw these away! They bring a fragrance to any soup and are essential in pea soup. Their freshness is perfect with eggs, chicken, tuna or meats.**

Chives: **Their delicate onion flavour goes with everything—except desserts!**

Mint: **This fresh herb works beautifully in all kinds of internationally inspired dishes, from India to England via the Maghreb. It also goes well with goat cheese and can flavour a number of desserts.**

Dill: **Incorporate some dill into cream or cheese when serving fish, seafood or eggs. It can also be used with celeriac, beets, cucumber, cabbage and corn.**

Tarragon: **Delicious with poultry, green beans, broccoli, beets, fennel (especially in a fennel salad with orange), seafood and even with certain fruits such as peaches.**

Thyme, rosemary, sage and lavender: **These work well with all red meats, squash and root vegetables. Infuse honey with them for a fantastic topping for cheese or fruit.**

Oregano: **Can be found in all the dishes that evoke Italy and the Mediterranean.**

Verbena (a rare herb, but I love it): **I use it with fennel and carrots, as well as with fruit and all kinds of desserts, and of course to fall asleep with . . .**

×

—

Thank you to Kirsten Hanson for believing in this book from the start, and to the good team at HarperCollins Canada. Thanks to Jessica Echenberg, who worked at Soupesoup a long time ago and also translated these recipes. Thanks to Katie Kostiuk, who perfectly translated the introduction.

Thank you to Dominique Lafond: I knew from the beginning that working together would be a pleasure. To Anne-Saskia Barthe, who put all her heart into this book. To Louise Loiselle, for her confidence in me. To Annie Lachapelle from Atelier Chinotto for her sense of style and grace.

Thank you to Sylvain Lafleur, a free spirit who has greatly contributed to this book and to Soupesoup. Thank you to the kitchen staff: Brigitte Lastrade, Robert Barboza, Carmelle Bonetto, Jean-Manuel Costela, France Quirion, and to my favourite accountant, Stéphane Lessard.

Thank you to Elias Malouf, who has always supported me over the years. To Joseph Hillel, who had the initial idea for a soup restaurant. Thank you to Marie Blouin, Sonia Vigneault, Michelle Blouin, Denis Blouin and Annie Dumas, who always had faith. Thank you to my grocer with a big heart, Julia Soares.

Thank you to Henri Cleinge, for his pure, architectural genius at all the Soupesoup locations. To Nicolas Bonetto, craftsman of exquisite tables. To Jimmy Deschênes, artist with many talents. To Bernard Lanteigne, discoverer of beautiful objects. To Éric Barbeau, who conceived the restaurant design of Soupesoup on Duluth. To Eva Van Den Bulcke, who created the logo for Soupesoup.

Thank you to my business partners: Roger Frappier, Caroline Desgagné, Julie Bernard, Rochelle Sarre, Neulis Perez and Jean Fugère.

Thank you to the team at Zone3: Brigitte Lemonde, Michel Bissonnette, Vincent Leduc, André Larin and Luc Rousseau. Thank you to France Castel, who is both vivacious and generous, and to the delightful Michel Barrette. To the adorable and delicious Marc Maula. To Lisa Birri for all of her kindness. To Lucie Denis and Blaise Renaud for their incredible confidence in me. To Patrice Roy, for having devoted an entire show to me—it was like winning a prize!

An infinite thank you to Rachel Bernard, my grandmother who left me her famous recipe for *pouding chômeur*—the same one that Martin Picard tasted at Soupesoup and put on the menu at his restaurant to everyone's delight!

Thank you to my mother, Thérèse Rodrigue, and her large family, which nurtured my childhood. Uncle Gérald Duval, who, unknowingly, challenged me to make soup as good as his! My eighty cousins, whom I have not seen for a long time but who fill my memories of laughter and special times together.

To Roger, my companion, who takes me as I am. To my two beautiful daughters, for having chosen me as their mother: this is your first cookbook!

×

Alicia / Carine / Benoît / Bob / Carla / Dorothée / Emma / Francesco / Gilberto / Gino / Janie / Kim / Leah / Marie-Justine / Marie-Mai / Nadja / Naomie / Norma / Numa / Sunny / Virginie / Yatik / Yohan / Barbara Adly / Johanne Ahelo / Alexis Ahelo-White / Malin Anagrius / Claudette Anglade / John Ashmore / Christian Aubry / Juliette Aubry / Pascal Auclair / Dominique Babin / Karim Babin / Martin Balthazar / Éric Barbeau / Robert Barboza / Marie Barguirdjian / Audrey Baril / Guillaume Barre / Michel Barrette / Anne-Saskia Barthe / Gloria Basso / Charles Beauchemin / Robert Beauchemin / Camille Béland-Goyette / Éric Bélanger / Philippe Bélanger / Sonia Belgaid / Sylvie Bercowicz / Philémon Bergeron-Langlois / Julie Bernard / Rachel Bernard / Éric Bernier / François Berthiaume / Janette Bertrand / Guylaine Bérubé / Alain Besré / Bruno Birri / Lisa Birri / Nino Birri / Michel Bissonnette / Marc-André Blanchard / Léonie Blanchet / Denis Blouin / Marie Blouin / Michelle Blouin / Dominique Bodkin / Antoine Bonetto / Carmelle Bonetto / Nicolas Bonetto / Brigitte Bouchard / Simon Bouffard / Benoît Brière / Dean Brisson / Michel Brisson / Sandrina Bucci / Anne-Marie Cadieux / Geneviève Cadieux / Sarah Canta / Léa-Marie Cantin / Pierre-Jacob Carillo / Laurence Carmant / Camille Caron-Belzile / Ian Cart / Jérémie Casabon / France Castel / Marilyn Castonguay / Laurent Chabot / Manon Chaput / Florence Charest / Robert Charpentier / François Chénier / Marylène Chrétien / Éric Cinq-Mars / Henri Cleinge / Frédéric Cloutier / Antoine Cloutier-Fugère / Geneviève Cocke / Lou Cogne / Henri Cohen / Lucille Colas / Ellen Corin / Claude Cormier / Jean-François Cormier / Jean-Manuel Costela / Marc-Antoine Coulombe / Antonello Cozzolino / Alain Cusson / Nicolle Dallaire / Cristiano Da Silva / Jacques Davidts / Alexandre de Barcelona / Richard Deguire / François Delisle / Claude Demers / Michel Demers / Lucie Denis / Marie-Michelle Deschamps / Jimmy Deschênes / Serge Deschênes / Caroline Desgagné / Lhasa de Sela / Claude Despins / Ève Déziel / Brigitte Dion / Pietro di Monaco / Josée di Stasio / Constantina Doanis / Marie Dory / Sophie Doval / Richard Doyon / Laurence Dubois / Chantal Dufresne / Annie Dumas / Clara Florence Dumas / Jean-François Dumas / Maurice Dumas / Maxime Dumas / Odette Dumas / Alexia Dumas-Malouf / Francine Duquette / Gérald Duval / Jessica Echenberd / Isabelle Émond / Hinda Essadiqi / Jean-Jacques Fauchois / Marie-Odile Fauchois / Odette Fauchois / Véronique Fauchois / François Fauteux / Jean-Pierre Fauteux / Pascale Ferland / Rafael Fernandez / Thomas Fersen / Iso Fiddes / Jean Fillion / Aube Foglia / Manuel Foglia / Ashley Ford / Dominique Fortier / Jean Fortin / Félize Frappier / Renée Frappier / Roger Frappier / Vincent Frappier / Jean Fugère / Michel Gaudette / Claire Geoffrion / Zoé Geoffrion-Sanders / Chloé Germain-Fredette / Bertrand Giguère / Huguette Gilbert / Olivia Gionet-Bouchard / Claude Girard / Claude-Antoine Girard / Sofie Girouard / Laure Goudeault / Olivier Gourde / Hedi Graja / Lucie Grandet / Rachel Graton / Nathalie Grégoire / Catherine Grégoire-Couillard / Brigitte Haentjens / Patrick Hamilton / Christine Harvey / Geneviève Hébert / Joseph Hillel / Binky Holleran / Sheena Hoszko / Éric Houle / Ian Hovelaque / Clode Jalette / Daniel Janson / Jana Jevtonic / Mauve-Lune Jolly / Nicole Labbé / Catherine Lachance / Annie Lachapelle / Sylvia Landa / Sylvain Lafleur / Dominique Lafond / Line Lafontaine / Nicolas Landry / Bernard Lanteigne / Steve Lapierre / Jacqueline Laporte / Robin Laporte / Normand Laprise / Stéphanie Larichelière / André Larin / Ninon Laroche / Patrick Larrivée / Alexis Lastrade / Brigitte Lastrade / Louise Latraverse / Johanne Latreille / Rosalie Lavoie / François Lebel / Mathilde Leblanc / Sophie Leblond / Vincent Leduc / Jean-Philippe Lefebvre / Julien Lelièvre / Brigitte Lemonde / France Léonard / Lison Lescarbeau / Stéphane Lessard / Jade Lévesque-Rivard / Macha Limonchik / Julien Livernois / Louise Loiselle / Perrine Lotiron / Dany Madani / Laure Mallet / Fanny Mallette / Frank Mally / Elias Malouf / Frédéric Mamarbachi / Brigitte Marchand / Nino Marcone / Alexis Martin / Stéphanie Martin / Marc Maula / Leslie Mavangui / Gaspard Mazzola / Camille McOuat / Yves Médam / Johanne Ménard / Mario Mercier / François Méthé / Mylène Millie / Reinier Monteagudo-Gutierrez / Sylvia-Laura Morales / Sophie Moreau / Véronique Moreau / Line Nault / Roxanne Néron / Tram Nguyen / Florence Noyer / Michèle Ouellette / Carol Painchaud / Anna Palmetsofer / Alexis Papadumitriou / Maryse Paré / Pascale Paroissien / Alice Pascual / Fernando Peireira / Véronica Pelivaric / Angie Pelletier / Andréa Peplow / Neulis Perez-Puebla / Stélio Perombelon / Nathalie Perron / Laurence Petterson / Jocelyn Picard / Martin Picard / Mylène Pratt / Alexis Pratte / Julien Pratte / Olivier Pratte / Christian Pronovost / Sébastien Puel / Stéphane Quintal / France Quirion / Julie Racine / Linda Ramsey / Lucas Rebick / Marianne Rehder / Rebecca Rehder / Blaise Renaud / Line Richer / Jean-Claude Rivard / Thérèse Rodrigue / Francis Rollin / Damien Rougier / Anne-Louise Rouleau / Bernard Rouleau / Johanne Rouleau / Martin Rouleau / Luc Rousseau / Pascale Roussin / Linda Roy / Nathalie Roy / Patrice Roy / Martine Royer / Maral Saghaie / Olivier Saint-Pierre / Pierre Sangra / Olga Saraguro / Rochelle Sarre / Catherine Sauvé / Luc Sergerie / Reema Singh / Jean-François Smith / Julia Soares / Geneviève Soly / Sarah Spring / Andréa Sproule / Gabrielle Steiger / Hadas Steiner / Dominic Sylvain / Martin Talbot / Dominic Tambuzzo / Jean-Philippe Tastet / Chantal Therrien / Pierre Therrien / Josée Thibault / Emmanuelle Tizon / Christian Tomov / Jimmy Tousignant / Hieu Tran / Thomas-Fionn Tran / Nancy Tremblay / Hélène Tremblay / Yannick Truesdale / Anne-Marie Trussart / Carl Valiquette / Geneviève Vallières / Eva Van Den Bulcke / Sonia Vigneault / Justine Villemaire / Karim Waked / Marilou Wilke / Francis Zerbid / Yvette Zerbid